"In the Paschal Mystery, the cross
occupies the visible and decisive part
which we can know and meditate
upon: it is the meeting-point of guilt
and innocence, the battle between
cruelty and goodness, the duel between
death and life. But it is also the
combination of justice and mercy,
the ransoming of pain through hope,
the triumph of love in sacrifice."

(Pope Paul VI, General Audience, September 15, 1971)

Msgr. Giulio Ricci

THE WAY OF THE CROSS IN THE LIGHT OF THE HOLY SHROUD

Roman Center of Sindonology

''Pilate took Jesus and scourged him'' (Jn 19:1).

To order more copies:
    Holy Shroud Center
    2647 Brunswick Ct.
    Lisle, IL 60532

CONTENTS

This publication on the Shroud is intentionally not a book of prayers, even though it illustrates a devotional practice of Christian piety—the Way of the Cross. It is, however, a book which incites us to prayer.

I had frequently been urged to translate the results of recent studies on the Shroud into pictorial form for purposes of devotion, and to present a realistic representation of the Way of the Cross according to the Gospels, amplified by archeological findings on the crucifixion and especially by findings from recent investigations on the Shroud.

I am presenting a new and true vision of the passion of Christ, without indulging in those pietistic sentiments which have too often guided pen, chisel and paintbrush to present a sweetened picture of the suffering Christ in the greatest drama of history. In this new approach, there is little need to call on the resources of creative imagination, but merely to carry out careful investigations in order to reconstruct those objective facts which, I think, must be the basis for any literary or artistic inspiration concerning the passion of Christ.

A more logical arrangement of the Stations (Simon of Cyrene after the three falls, and Veronica immediately before the Crucifixion) leads to a fifteenth Station: that of the resurrection of Christ.

"Was it not necessary that Christ should suffer these things and enter into his glory?" (Lk 24:26)

In this perspective the paschal mystery is seen in its fullness and offers us the same luminous hope which was the source of exultation for St. Paul: "We were buried therefore with him by baptism into death; so that as Christ was raised from the dead by the glory of the Father, we too might walk in newness of life. For if we have been united with him in a death like his, we shall certainly be united with him in a resurrection like his. We know that our old self was crucified with him so that the sinful body might be destroyed, and we might no longer be enslaved to sin.... But if we have died with Christ, we believe that we shall also live with him" (Rom 6:4-6, 8).

This is the light which bursts forth from the most glorious tomb in history, a light which shines into every human tomb, where the mystical members of Christ, purified by the great tribulation of life, await, after death, in the bareness of the tomb, the final resurrection and the life which will have no end.

THE AUTHOR

"**I**f you release this man, you are not Caesar's friend" (Jn 19:12).
  "'Here is your King!'... 'Away with him, away with him, crucify him!'... 'Shall I crucify your King?'... 'We have no king but Caesar!'" (Jn 19:14-15)

"So...Pilate...took water and washed his hands before the crowd, saying, 'I am innocent of this righteous man's blood; see to it yourselves....' 'His blood be on us and on our children'" (Mt 27:24-25).

The water of political compromise became the betrayal of the known and proclaimed Truth, and signified the handing over of the Innocent One to ill-intentioned enemies: it became blood!

Historically this sad event was confined to a few Jews, even though they formed a cleverly manipulated crowd that day, and to a wavering Roman judge. However, the fingers pointed at him are innumerable: those of the entire human race which, because of the mystery of sin, which involves everyone, accuses him, the Innocent, Holy One, King by divine origin and by the right of conquest, and points at him the finger of accusation as a mock king, rendered powerless, ridiculed, humiliated, rejected, condemned. Moreover, he is mystically condemned by our sinful judgments when these are passed on the actions and intentions of any innocent man, *with whom* he identifies himself: "*As you did it to one of the least of these my brethren, you did it to me*" (Mt 25:40).

In fact, in him each man is our brother. Through this mysterious yet real presence of God in our neighbor, each of us can find his own hand among those of all generations, with the index finger pointing in condemnation, for over the course of centuries the water from Pilate's jug has become a *river*, added to by each one of us—a river of blood, of his blood.

In the overwhelming mystery of men who condemn the Incarnate Son of God to death, there is also room for those who *welcome* his blood *in blessing*— those who have been washed in the blood of the Lamb through the "great tribulation" (Rev 7:14). It was of these that Jesus spoke when he called them "blessed." Blessed when, like himself, they are persecuted for love of justice, or condemned (on condition that, together with him, they offer up this humiliation to the Father). The hands of those who suffer, even if in the past they were used to condemn, are now used *in offering*, held together by love to form an overflowing chalice, from which the blood of Christ flows down to redeem by means of the mystical stigmata of pain.

This is the silent offering of the suffering and persecuted Church; it is the offering of those who *make over* to Christ their bodies and souls to complete what is still lacking in the Passion of Christ, the Head of the Church, for their own sanctification and that of those sinful members for whom there is "still the hope of pardon" (St. Ignatius of Antioch).

In an unexpected way, the Holy Shroud gives us evidence of the *dreadful investiture* of this mocked royalty.

The whole of the cranium[1] shows signs of a remarkable crown woven from long thorns which, in accord with the Eastern custom for the coronation of kings, was placed not *around* but *on top of the head*, like a miter.

"*They plaited a crown of thorns and put it on his head, and put a reed in his right hand. And kneeling before him they mocked him, saying, 'Hail, King of the Jews!' and struck him with their hands.... And they spat upon him and took the reed and struck him on the head*" (Jn 19:2-3; Mt 27:29-30; Mk 15:17-19). The blood must have streamed down all over his face!

The Holy Shroud shows us a surprising fact in the imprint of the face: there are only *a few* trickles of blood, and these flow only either straight down or towards the right, and *never towards the left*. These trickles flowed while Jesus was on the cross, some from wounds still open from the crowning with thorns, others from the right side of the mouth. It is important to note that of the ten trickles of blood from the occiput, seven tend toward the left. (Those which flowed during the crowning with thorns can be seen transferred onto the linen cloth with which, according to an ancient tradition, a pious woman of Jerusalem wiped the face of Jesus before he was crucified.)

Was Jesus Still Wearing the Crown of Thorns Along the Way to Calvary and on the Cross?

From the Gospels and from the historical context of the trial of Jesus, it is clear that the crowning with thorns went beyond Roman penal procedure and was simply a *cruel joke* thought up by the soldiers of the Praetorium to exalt, in their own way, the royalty that Jesus had shortly before asserted during his trial in front of Pilate. It was after the "Ecce Homo!" that is, when Pilate showed Jesus to the people, with the intention of demonstrating that he had been given an exemplary punishment, that Jesus appeared with the many marks of

1. On that portion of the head in the center of the cloth, in the two imprints (frontal and dorsal), separated by that brief space in the epicranium area, where no imprint was made, owing to a fold in the cloth.

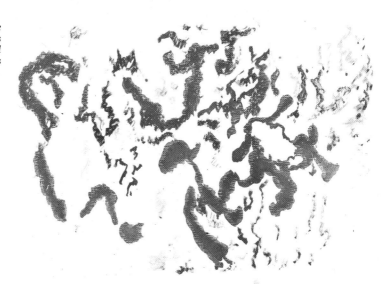

Skull of the Man of the Shroud showing numerous trickles of blood caused by a crowning with thorns

the scourging, dressed as a mock king with a purple mantle, and with a crown of thorns on his head. This crown must have made his face run with blood—that face which had already been beaten and punched, and made the target of spitting!

Pilate's intention to free Jesus, expressed twice before the scourging, crumbled at the prospect of being involved in a charge of rebellion against the emperor: "If you release this man, you are not Caesar's friend" (Jn 19:12). Thus Pilate decreed death on the cross for Jesus. At this point the episode of the crown of thorns ends, since, when Jesus had to put his own clothes back on (Mk 15:20) and be tied to the crosspiece for the painful journey, the bundle of thorns would have had to have been removed from his head.

No reliable historical source would allow one to state that the crown of thorns was put back on Jesus' head again. The only sources which would suggest this derive from artistic representations, and these are several centuries after the event. Likewise, there is no evidence that it was removed and put on again after Jesus had been stripped of his clothes on Calvary. Furthermore, the tunic, which was made in one piece with an opening at the neck, could not have been put on or removed without first having removed the crown.

*How the face of the fairest of the sons
of men must have appeared on
that first, sad Good Friday*

"*And he went out, bearing his own cross, to the place called the place of a skull''* (Jn 19:17).

At the time of Jesus, both in Rome and Jerusalem, those who had been sentenced to death on the cross had the crosspiece or *patibulum* tied behind their shoulders, with their arms outstretched. The *patibulum*[1] was a large wooden beam which, at the moment of execution, was placed in one of various ways onto the vertical stake which was already fixed into the ground.

Historians speak of the reluctance of these unfortunate condemned men, who struggled against being tied to the crosspiece, so that the use of force was needed to constrain them.[2] That day the two thieves must have behaved similarly.

Not so Jesus. "Oh! You should know with what sincere love the Creator of life welcomed this wood of the cross, not through force, but spontaneously!"[3] Jesus foretold this same *spontaneous* behavior for St. Peter, prophetically emphasizing, during his third apparition following the resurrection, that he would die by crucifixion as an expression of love: "Do you love me more than these?... Feed my lambs.... Feed my sheep.... When you are old, you will stretch out your hands, and another will gird you and carry you where you do not wish to go" (Jn 21:15-18). Thus, in imitation of him, Peter was to repeat in Rome the attitude of Jesus in Jerusalem. Jesus had given himself up *voluntarily* to the passion, with love and with no constraint. He, like his Vicar after him, spontaneously stretched out his arms to receive the wood of the cross.

The shoulders of the Man of the Shroud show two large imprints in the area of the left scapula and above the right scapula. The parallel lines drawn on the photograph on the following page show the slant of the *patibulum* (20°), the *stauròs* of the Synoptic Gospels and of St. John. The nature of the imprints should be mentioned: the contusion on the left scapula, which is more extensive than the other, shows that this area supported more of the weight of the wood than did the other area, higher up, which is less marked. This agrees with the fact that, in this case, the lower end of the crosspiece was *tied* to the left ankle. Any movement made by the Man of the Shroud while he was

---

1. From the Latin verb *patēre*, to open; it was the piece of wood placed in two openings in the thickness of a wall, which served to close and open doors, and which was used by masters to send rebellious slaves to be crucified.
2. Cf. Dionysius of Halicarnassus, *Hist. Rom.*, 7,69.
3. *P.G.*, II (Acts of the Martyrdom of St. Andrew).

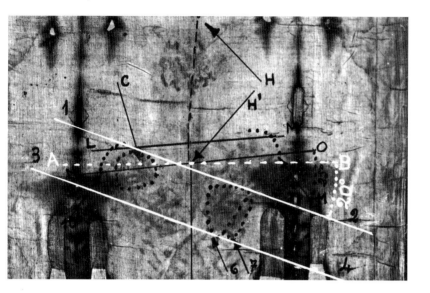

6–7, Area of the left scapula: *contusion caused by carrying the crosspiece tied to the shoulders. A slight extension of the contusion can be seen to the outside of the scapula; this must have occurred when the Man's arms were stretched out, tied to the crosspiece.*

walking would tend to make the crosspiece slip lower, and so weigh down even more on this area, while the other area would be eased.

It should also be mentioned that, in those areas marked by contact with the crosspiece, the marks of the scourging are also clearly visible. This unusual detail can be explained by the fact that *the shoulders of the Man of the Shroud were first struck by the whips,* and were then protected by clothes on the way to the place of crucifixion. In fact, had it not been for the clothes, the rough wood in contact with the skin would have notably opened the lacerations, and thus clearly altered the whip marks. We have seen from the trial of Jesus that he was scourged *before* being condemned to death, not to get him to talk, but as a "lesson" which was to serve him for the future...since he was to be freed (Lk 23:16, 20-22).

When Pilate decreed death with the chilling words: "You will go to the cross!" Jesus was again clothed in his own garments and was spared a second scourging, which was normally given to common criminals and was carried out along the way to the place of execution.

This surprising proof that a scourging was carried out before the crosspiece, tied to the shoulders, left its two well-known imprints, is supported by the geometry of the whip marks, which overall show two clear converging points, one focal point to the right and another to the left.[4] This corresponds with the scourging of a man in a stationary position, carried out by two Roman scourgers: the number of whip strokes (the whip had three thongs or cords which were weighted at the ends) far exceeds (there are over 121) the 40 strokes prescribed by Moses in Jewish law.

4. This has also been confirmed by the digital enhancement of the Holy Shroud images done by Dr. Lynn of Pasadena.

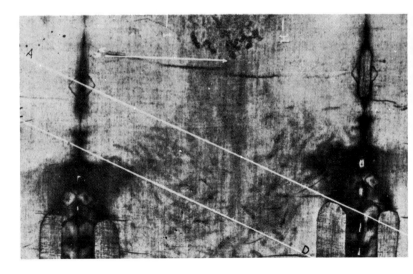

A – B and C – D show the oblique direction of the crosspiece tied to the shoulders of the Man of the Shroud

The Gospel story does not tell us that Jesus fell along the *via dolorosa,* nor does it mention the whipping of the two thieves who were to share the same punishment as the Lord. But their death, which had already been decreed, previous to and independent of the death of Jesus, was by custom preceded by being whipped, naked to the waist, along the way.

Thus the painful procession from the Antonia Tower begins with the scene of whips striking the two thieves at random, and with the sound of their curses and wild cries as they writhed under the blows.

It is easy to see the principal direct cause of the falls of the Man third in line: the top ends of the crosspieces were, for reasons of security, tied together by the rope[1]; also, Jesus had been made to put on his long garment again.

A real-life experiment

1. C. Cl. Licinius, *Hist. Rom. (Fragmenta* of Nonius), ed. Peter, 2,78.

At every stroke of the whip, the thieves must have writhed about, dragging and pushing each other. It was the Third of the condemned men who suffered from this. He had already been scourged and, stumbling along under the wood of the cross, he was forced to the ground.[2] The left leg, tied to the end of the crosspiece, gave way at the sudden tug, and the left knee struck violently against the paving stones of the roads of Jerusalem, while the heavy crosspiece, which before the fall was supported diagonally above the right shoulder blade, began to press down with all its weight on the left shoulder blade, already repeatedly struck by the whip. Jesus' hands were tied to the crosspiece, so he could not stop his face from striking the flagstones, while his only support (which was his sole means of avoid-

The seriously contused area —as shown by dots—corresponds to the outer part of the left knee. The right knee does not seem to show clear evidence of contusion; this would support the theory that the crosspiece was tied to the left foot, with consequences as described.

2. Recent experiments using actual beams tied to the arms and secured to the left ankle led *inevitably* to the man's falling as soon as the opposite end of the beam was tugged violently.

ing concussion of the brain) was the rope which tied his crosspiece to that of the nearer criminal.

This reconstruction, based on literary historical texts, and confirmed in several ways by close study of the Shroud, supports the Christian tradition that Jesus fell at least three times along the *via dolorosa*.

The first feature on the Shroud which confirms this and which holds good for all the other possible falls (that is, up to the time when the crosspiece was untied from his shoulders, after which his manner of walking changed completely) is to be found in the lacerated contusions on the left knee of the Man of the Shroud.

The other features are to be found in the various contusions on the face *which inevitably suffered the consequences of the impact.* The *first* of these features I see in the swelling on the left brow and cheekbone, and I associate it with the first fall. Compared to the other swellings on the face, these seem the least serious; and, as the agony of the situation would have become progressively more overwhelming, right up to the point where it was thought advisable to untie the crosspiece from Jesus' shoulders, I attribute it to the *first* fall.

The left brow and cheekbone with signs of bruising

21

The humiliating fall which suddenly brought Jesus of Nazareth to the ground, face downwards, must have had a deep effect on the heart of one particular person who was watching him from among the crowd: Mary of Nazareth, his Mother! The sword of suffering prophesied by the holy old man Simeon (Lk 2:35) was penetrating ever more deeply into her soul.

The hour of the sorrowful redemption had struck, and she too had to be there, having consented freely, when asked by God through the Archangel Gabriel, to the Incarnation of the Son of God for the "salvation of his people."

She must have made that most natural gesture—as shown in the illustration—which must have touched the soldiers and the crowd: a motherly caress on that beautiful face, so disfigured by blows, slaps, punches, spittle, and also now by that first fall. She lays her right hand gently on the left brow and cheek which has been so badly hurt by the impact with the stones. The consolation must have been reciprocal. The silent, but eloquent, language of their countenances resounds with perfect obedience to the will of the Father: "Lo, I have come to do thy will" (Heb 10:9). "Behold, I am the handmaid of the Lord; let it be to me according to your word" (Lk 1:38). And the offertory of the first bloody sacrifice mingles with that of her who for thirty-three years had been preparing the pure, holy and immaculate Host for humanity.

To most of the onlookers, the presence of the Mother of him who was accursed by official Judaism of the day and condemned to death must have seemed very humiliating for her also. To those few friends, on the other hand, who did not see her beside her Son when the crowd shouted their hosannas and acclaimed him, wanting him as their king, she must now have seemed most noble and lovable.

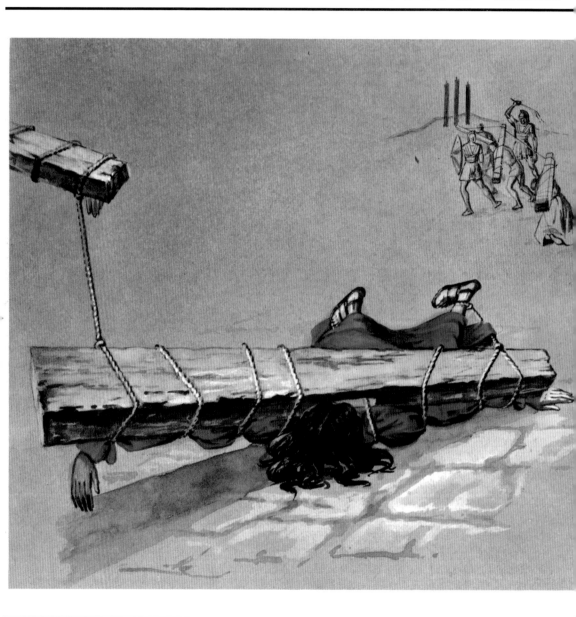

A second fall can be "read" on the face of the Shroud in a remarkable swelling in the middle of the forehead and in the fracture of the nasal septum. When the Shroud was brought into contact with the forehead, it did not touch the sides of the forehead; the swelling in the middle came into contact with the material and left its imprint there, while the adjacent areas are shaded. According to the judgment of experts, between the edge of the nasal septum and the beginning of the cartilage, a concave area can be seen, indicative of a fracture caused by some blow.

Swelling in the middle of the forehead and the fractured nasal septum

The area above the *right* eyebrow and on the right cheekbone must have suffered the main shock of this last fall which was undoubtedly very violent, as even the strength of the other condemned men must have been waning by that time. The swelling resulting from the violent contusion has so disfigured the right eye as to make it unrecognizable.

Swellings over the whole area of the right eye socket

Following pages:
Positive and negative photographs of the face of the Man of the Shroud

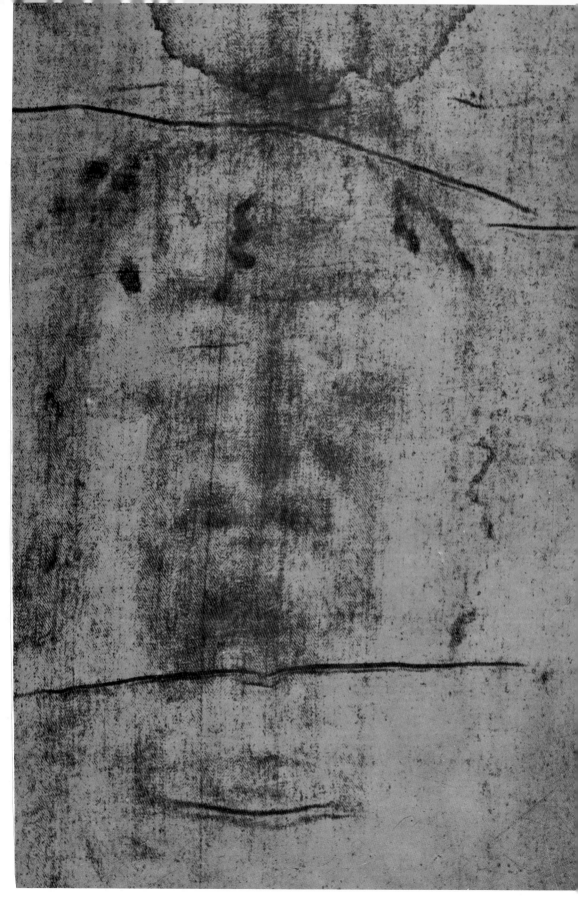

"As they were marching out, they came upon a man of Cyrene, Simon by name, the father of Alexander and Rufus, who was coming in from the country; this man they compelled to carry his cross" (Mk 15:21; Mt 27:32).

Such a serious decision—unique in the history of crucifixions—that of lifting the crosspiece from the shoulders of the condemned Man in order to allow him to reach the Place of the Skull alive, must have been taken because of his serious state of physical exhaustion, and also because they did not want to see him die ignominiously by the wayside. It was taken, in effect, because of a false compassion in order to satisfy the cruelty of Jesus' enemies, who wanted at all costs to see him die on the cross.

From a medical point of view, the face of the Man of the Shroud appears seriously injured and disfigured. Apart from the bruising already mentioned and the fracture of the nasal cartilage, both directly caused by the falls along the wayside, that face had previously undergone other injuries. On the right cheek, on a level with the lower part of the nose, a large swelling is visible, which brings to mind a violent blow from a stick. Another sign of a similar blow can be seen in the swelling visible in the center of the forehead, where the trickle of blood in the shape of a "3" begins.

Experts also draw attention to the swollen upper right lip and to the chin.[1] Doctors do not exclude the possibility that the condemned Man might have collapsed through cerebral shock if these conditions had been repeated.

When the beam was untied from his shoulders and given to Simon of Cyrene,[2] Jesus was still lying on the ground, tied by the ankle. He must have been helped to his feet in order to continue on his arduous journey. Meanwhile the Cyrenian looked on with tears in his eyes, and willingly embraced[3] the heavy beam which he carried loose on his shoulders as far as Calvary.

1. Gedda, *La Passione di Cristo secondo la Sindone*, in *Tabor*, V, 1950, pp. 513-547.
2. The oldest pictures of the Way of the Cross (15th and 16th centuries) show Simon "helping" Jesus to carry the cross, holding the end of the longer upright beam, but leaving the rest of the cross on the shoulders of Jesus. (15th century: H. Multscher, 1400-1467; and the miniaturists Jean and Paul De Limbourg, Cristoforo de Predis, and Maestro di Albrecht. 16th century: Allori, 1535-1607, and many others.) This false artistic exegesis has led to the justification of the second and third falls of Jesus "under the cross" at a time when it was in reality, according to the Gospels, on the shoulders of Simon.
3. The original meaning of the verb used by the evangelists, *angariaverunt*, is "requisition, commandeer," i.e., to compel someone to work without payment, which does not necessarily indicate, as in this case, any reluctance on the part of the man of Cyrene.

"**A**nd there followed him a great multitude of the people, and of women who bewailed and lamented him. But Jesus turning to them said, 'Daughters of Jerusalem, do not weep for me; but weep for yourselves and for your children. For behold, the days are coming when they will say, "Blessed are the barren, the wombs that never bore, the breasts that never gave suck!" Then they will begin to say to the mountains, "Fall on us"; and to the hills, "Cover us." For if these things are done when the wood is green, what will happen when it is dry?'

"Two others also, who were criminals, were led away to be put to death with him" (Lk 23:27-32).

HIS GARMENTS

"Then they cast lots to divide his garments'' (Lk 23:34).

In the area of the flexory muscle of the radial carpus of the left forearm can be seen some trickles of blood which run in similar directions to those on the same hand. However, while the two little trickles—at an angle of about 35° to each other—from the nailhole in the left wrist illustrate the two painful movements of sagging and raising up, those on the radial carpus were probably reopened when the soldiers pulled off Jesus' clothing. In fact, that part of the forearm would have been pressed tightly against the cloth because of the way the beam had been bound.

When the beam was untied, the clothes would have stuck to the wounds until they were removed. Since he was put on the cross immediately, the small amount of blood which oozed from the wounds flowed down in two clearly differentiated directions, similar to those on the wrist.

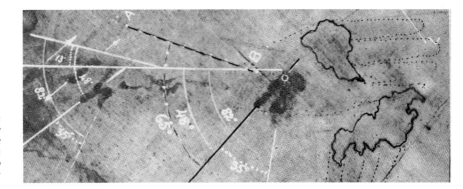

Left forearm of the Man of the Shroud with the trickles of blood in parallel position to those from the wrist

A feature of the Holy Shroud worthy of examination is the direction of the trickles of blood on the nape of the neck of the Man of the Shroud as compared with those on the face. There is clear disagreement, in that those on the neck almost all run towards the left, while the few that are shown on the face run straight down or to the right and never to the left.

This simple observation can logically lead us to deduce that before the crucifixion some merciful hands wiped his face; this pious action was, however, confined to the face, and did not include the back of the neck.

This observation from the Holy Shroud may help to authenticate another relic which very old tradition attributes to a pious woman of Jerusalem on whose linen cloth the imprint of Jesus' face remained when she wiped it before he was crucified. Clearly these bloodstains will not be the same as those that characterize the face on the Shroud, since the latter were caused *after* he was taken down from the cross and bear witness to the two movements of sagging and raising up with which He began the painful three hours' agony.

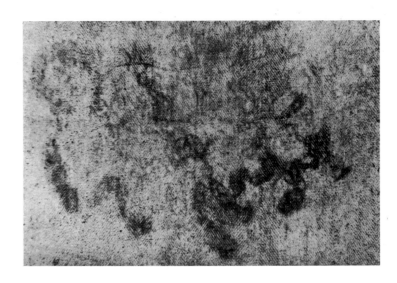

Traces of blood on the occiput from the crowning with thorns; the majority flow to the left

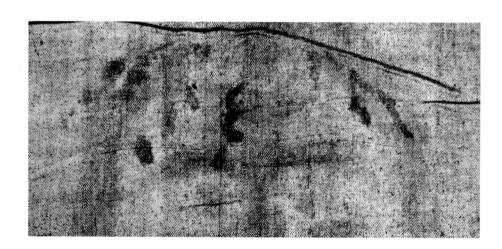

Traces of blood on the forehead of the Man of the Shroud from the crowning with thorns.
They flow in two directions (vertical and to the right), in keeping with
the two positions of the head at the beginning of the agony on the cross when
it would appear he underwent the two states of sagging downwards
(vertical flow of blood) and raising up, with a relative movement to the right (flow of blood
to the right). Contrary to what is found on the occiput, here there is no flow to the left.

G. RICCI: Study for a ''Pietà''

"**A**nd he went out, bearing his own cross, to the place called the place of the skull, which is called in Hebrew Golgotha. There they crucified him with two others, one on either side, and Jesus between them" (Jn 19:17-18). "They have pierced my hands and feet" (Ps 21:16).

The crucifixion, as is shown by analytical study of the Holy Shroud, reveals how cruel this method of execution was. He was crucified in such a way as to accelerate death.

Ropes or nails could be used to crucify, and sometimes a piece of wood, like a seat, was put between the legs in order to prolong life.

In the case of the Man of the Shroud, the wound from a nail in the left wrist is evident. This is the first remarkable detail revealed about this crucifixion. Almost all artists, from the Byzantine period until today, have placed the nail in the palm of the hand. It has been proved by experiment[1] that if an arm is nailed up by the palm of the hand and a weight of 40 kilograms (about 88 pounds) is attached to it, after ten minutes the hand gives way under the weight and tears away from the nail. The Romans, who were accustomed to this mode of execution, knew quite well that if they wanted to attach someone securely to the cross, the nail had to be placed either in the wrist or in the space between the radius and the ulna (the distal region).[2] In the case of the

1. Barbet, *La Passion de N.S. Jesus Christ selon le chirurgien*, Dillen, Issaudun, 1950.
2. Plautus, *Mostellaria*, act. 2, scene 1, vv. 12, 13.

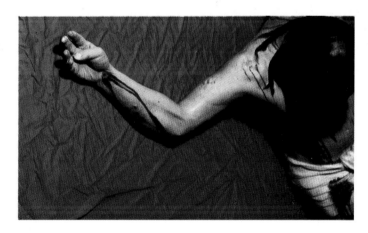

*The Crucifix of Assisi
(Regional Seminary
of Pius XI):
detail of right arm*

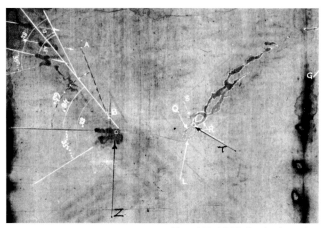

Z and T: *Nailholes in the wrists*

Man of the Shroud, the wrist was chosen and the nail was hammered into the so-called destot space, where it met the median nerve. This nerve is both sensory, so that when injured it causes excruciating shooting pains, and motor, affecting the movement of the thumb through the thenar muscles. Medical experiments have shown that as soon as a nail is inserted into a wrist, even into a recently amputated one, the thumb is drawn over into the palm of the hand. This would explain why the imprint of the left hand of the Man of the Shroud shows only four fingers and no thumb.

As concerns the feet, it is the right one which clearly shows signs of a nail in the upper part (4) and in the sole of the second metatarsal area (see following page). From this wound there are trickles of blood running in several directions, in accordance with the rotary movement which the

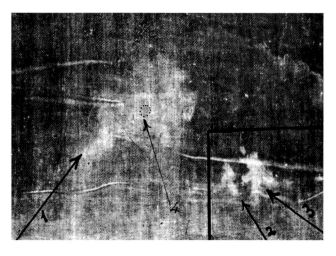

1–4: *The rose-shaped bloodstain, in the center of which is seen the nail hole. Its oblique form and the fact that it covers the upper side of the foot combine to show that the left foot was laid over the right.*

foot would presumably be forced to make in the effort to support the body.

On the upper part of the foot, however, the nail hole is surrounded by a large bloodstain which covers the whole of the foot—a clear sign that the left foot was over the right. Thus, reproducing on the sole of the left foot the reversed imprint of the rose-shaped bloodstain found on the top of the right foot, we will have found the position of the nail hole.

If we work out the shifting movement, we discover another surprising detail, which is shown as no. 5 on the sketch below.

It is obvious that the nail which bore the weight of the body of the Crucified Man caused particular damage to the area immediately surrounding it and that here a fold formed in the skin and filled with blood. When the nail was removed, the blood which had recently collected in that area was very easily absorbed by the sheet.

The only trace shown on the sole of the left foot on the Shroud of Turin is the heel and an oblique bloodstain immediately above the nail hole.

Let us now take a look at the sketch drawn over the photograph of the left foot:

1, 2 and 3: fingerprints of someone who carried the body;

4: the *rose-shaped bloodstain* found on the upper surface of the right foot, which during the crucifixion was in contact with the sole of the left foot, is *copied in reverse* over the latter;

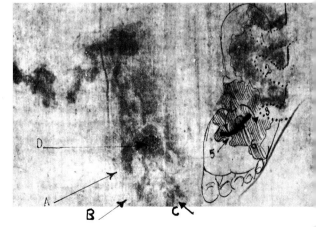

Imprint of the soles of the feet. A, B and C: trickles of blood apparently caused by rotary movement of the right foot. D: nail hole in the sole of the right foot

Basilica of Santa Croce
in Gerusalemme (Rome):
reproduction of the relic
of the "accusation" from the cross
with the word "Nazarene" in Greek,
Latin and, partly, in Aramaic

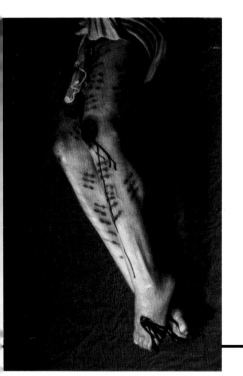

Crucifix of Assisi
(Regional Seminary of Pius XI):
detail of the feet

5: a trickle of blood, the oblique direction of which seems to follow a fold in the skin caused by the proximity of the nail which bore the weight of the body;

6: nail hole corresponding to the one on the right foot.

If the right foot had been nailed separately from the left, there would only have been trickles of blood and not a mass of blood with the mark of the nail in the middle.

The Shroud satisfies our curiosity through the eloquence of its imprints, showing that three and not four nails were used to crucify Jesus.

John of Ezechiel: A Man Crucified in Jerusalem

On the 4th of January, 1971, the sensational discovery was announced of the skeleton of a man crucified at the time of Jesus. The discovery was made at the Giv'at ha – Mivtar Cemetery by Professor Nicu Haas, anthropologist at the University of Jerusalem.[3]

The discovery consists of the remains of the bones of a certain John of Ezechiel, aged between 24 and 28 years, and show the man to have been 1.67 meters tall (or 5 feet 5¾ inches). The nails in the arms are situated in the distal region (between the ulna and the radius), while in the feet a single nail, about 17 cm. (6¾ inches) long, has pierced the two heels, which were placed side by side. "The right foot," says Professor Haas, "was the first to be pierced by the nail, that was protruding about 2.5 cm. (1 inch) in front of the left. This shows that the feet were side by side even on the cross."[4]

The head of the nail stuck out about 2 cm. (0.79 of an inch) from the heel bone. The space between was filled by a small acacia or pistachio wood the remains of which still cling to the nail and which must have been used to ensure the fixing of the feet and—according to Professor Haas—*to show the name of the condemned man.*

3. *Israel Exploration Journal*, XX (1971), pp. 38-59.

4. John of Ezechiel has shown the feet nailed in such a way that the left foot is nailed first, not the right, contrary to what Professor Haas has stated, as is clear from the illustration on page 56 of his article. Here the nail has been inserted horizontally between the heel and ankle bone of the right foot.

It is pertinent here to note that the "accusation" of Jesus was placed *"over his head"* (Mt 27:37), and not at his feet as was apparently the more normal custom according to the recent discoveries. The fact that this execution was to be an "example" evidently also suggested this refinement, emphasized in the evangelist's historical account.

Laboratory examination revealed the presence of fragments of knot-grained olive wood at the end of the nail, which was bent by the toughness of the wood. Professor Nicu Haas adds: "The position imposed on the body, the diagonal entry of the main nail, and the fact that by chance the point of the nail met a knot in the olive wood, together caused the nail to bend and emerge from the wood a little way (1 or 2 cm., or 0.39 or 0.79 of an inch). Analysis of the nail shows that it was initially between 17 and 18 cm. (about 7 inches) long, enough to pierce the two heelbones and to ensure that it stayed firmly in the wood. Actually, after the shaft of the nail had bent, the total length of a nail in a straight line was only 12 cm. (4½ inches). The fact that the nailhead stuck out from the edge of the right heel by 2 cm. (0.79 of an inch), and that the thin wooden plaque was straight when found, suggests that the nail was not firmly fixed into the wood of the cross" (p. 58).

As we can see, the method of crucifixion for the Man of the Shroud was considerably different as regards the position of the nails in the hands and feet. This is hardly surprising, since the way in which a crucifixion was carried out was not an unalterable "rite" but was subject to the whim of the executioners.[5]

A comparison of the two crucifixions would show that a more subtle cruelty was employed in the case of the Man of the Shroud than was the case for John of Ezechiel. The interesting point here is the difference in the position of the nail in the feet. In Jesus' case, the feet were not brought together side by side but placed one above the other, and pierced by a single nail through the second metatarsal space. The fact that the raising up movement of the body was considerable, as shown by a geometric study of the Shroud, leads one to suppose that at the moment of crucifixion the knees were considerably bent. The movements were possible because of the absence of any support at the perineum, and they must have been a feature of the first moments of the agony, leading to such comments, shouted by his enemies under the cross, as: "He saved others; he cannot save himself!" meaning: "However hard you try,

---

5. Jos. Flav., *B.J.*, Bk. V, 451.

you can't manage to save yourself!" These movements would certainly have produced an indescribable agony through their effect on the median nerve—a pain which John of Ezechiel must have been spared.

Because of the support at the perineum and the position of the nail in the feet, John would have found it physically impossible to make any noticeable movement, and his death at sunset must have been hastened by the breaking of the tibiae *(crurifragium)*, which has been proved.

In the controversy raised by the discovery of the remains of John of Ezechiel, there has been a tendency to try to reduce all crucifixions of that time to the model of the one under examination: Jesus' crucifixion, it is said, must have been carried out in the same way, as also the crucifixion of the thieves; in fact, some people have identified John of Ezechiel with one of the thieves crucified with Jesus.

If we did not have the testimony of an eyewitness, Josephus Flavius, who tells us that in the year 70, during the siege of Jerusalem, the crucifixions (about five hundred per day) were carried out in "various ways" by the Roman soldiers ("As a mark of their contempt, the soldiers would crucify the Jewish prisoners in various positions."[6]), this would not have been an unreasonable supposition.

In the case of Jesus, there is an interesting confirmation given by Professor Nicu Haas himself. He recognizes the position of the nails in the wrists as being a feature supporting the authenticity of the Shroud, but considers that the position of the nail in the feet could not be authentic because, supposing the existence of a nail in the metatarsus (as in the case of the Man of the Shroud), death would have followed only a few hours later—yet this is precisely what did happen to Jesus.

In fact, Jesus was put on the cross at about the sixth hour (midday) (Mt 27:45-46), and died at the ninth hour (3 p.m.). Furthermore, Pilate's surprise is a witness to the fact that the ruthlessness of this particular crucifixion must have been such as to cut short the agony. The absence of the support at the perineum, shown by the Shroud, the bent knees, and the position of the nails in the wrists and central metatarsus, are further proof of this. Consequently, there was no breaking of the legs, since the crucified Man was dead scarcely three hours after the crucifixion.

6. *Ibid.*, Bk. V, 450.

If we wish to speak of the death of Christ, we should follow the Holy Gospels faithfully, and add to this a careful reading of that historical document, the Holy Shroud. Both, without any doubt, speak of Jesus of Nazareth.

I would be more cautious in identifying John of Ezechiel with one of the thieves. The breaking of the legs was common to all crucified men who (at Jerusalem, though not at Rome) had to be killed if they were still alive at sunset on Friday, lest the land be defiled by the body (cf. Deut 21:23).

If one wanted to argue from the findings of laboratory examination, namely, the presence of granular particles of olive wood still attached to the point of the nail, one would recall the testimony of Josephus Flavius, who tells us how all the trees (which were mainly olive) within a large radius of Jerusalem had been cut down for the crucifixion of the Jews who did not surrender or who were captured outside the walls during the siege. If the corpses were requested, they were always handed over: there is the well-known case of a friend of Josephus Flavius who, crucified but still alive, was personally requested by him from the Emperor Titus, who granted the request.

Furthermore, while the most ancient Christian tradition speaks of ropes being used for the thieves, the Gospels would also not lead one to believe that the thieves had nails in their wrists, as did John of Ezechiel, precisely because of the nature of their words from the cross, which are psychologically incompatible with men whose median nerves are torn by nails. Besides this, there are a number of explicit references (Xenophontos of Ephesus—2nd century A.D.— refers to the Egyptian custom of crucifixion with ropes as being the local custom also) concerning other crucifixions at the time of Jesus; for one of these, ropes and not nails were used, "*so that,*" it is said, "*he might live longer,*" as was the case for the crucifixion of St. Andrew. The thieves, who arrived at Calvary naked, whipped and tied to the crosspiece, were by then ready for the final stage—the insertion of the crosspiece into the upright post already fixed in the ground.

The support at the buttocks or perineum (according to St. Justin) and the tying of the feet simplified the final stage of the method. Not so for Jesus, who arrived at Calvary without the crosspiece on his shoulders and dressed in his own garments. Once he was stripped, the decision was made on the spot: and the choice was nails.

*The nail, with bent tip,
which pierced the heels,
placed side by side,
of John of Ezechiel*

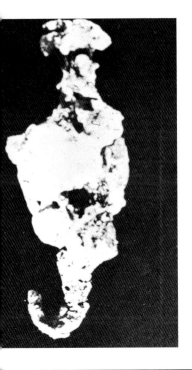

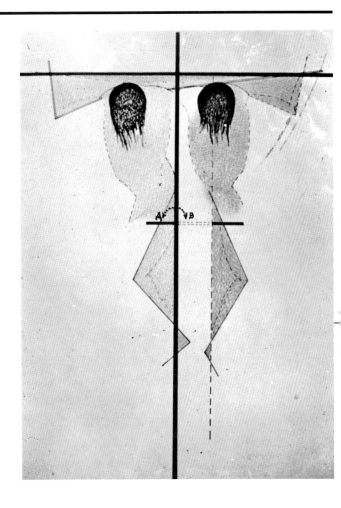

*Sketch of the support at the perineum
as used in some crucifixions. The different
directions taken by the trickles of blood
on the forearms exclude the use of such
a support in the case of the Man of the Shroud.*

The three-hour agony of Jesus would lead us to believe that the crucifixion of our Lord must have been carried out in such a way as to allow him to lift himself up considerably by pressing on the nail in the feet. In this way, he would have avoided almost immediate asphyxiation, and subsequently would have been able to breathe almost normally and to speak and cry out for some time, albeit with increasing difficulty as time passed.

This theory finds surprising confirmation in conclusions drawn from a geometric examination of the two converging trickles of blood on the left wrist. Examination shows the two positions that this body must have assumed: the one *sagging downwards* and the other *raised up*.

The first position, in which the body hung mainly from the arms, can be reconstructed by calculating the angle of the first trickle of blood in relation to the left forearm.

The second position (raised up) is so shown by the 35° angle formed by a second blood trickle with the first, starting from the same nail hole.

This rotary movement of the forearms caused two extensive contusions of the metacarpal crown or upper sides of the hands, which were violently pressed against the wood of the cross. The fulcrum of these movements was the nail in the wrist. Thus the forearms were transformed into two levers.

To understand correctly the effects of this rotary movement on the hands of the Man of the Shroud, two facts should be borne in mind: (1) in the raising up movement the body was pushed forward because of the position of the feet which were nailed one over the other; (2) the right forearm underwent a greater rotary movement because of the nature of the vertical position assumed in the shift to the right.

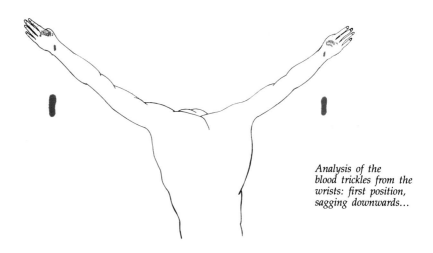

Analysis of the blood trickles from the wrists: first position, sagging downwards...

...first raised-up position...

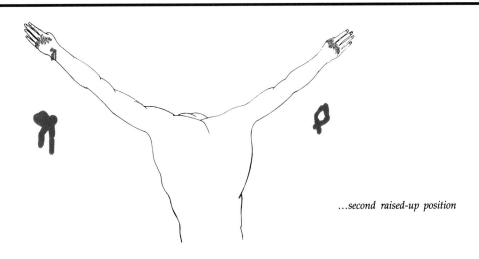

...second raised-up position

*...second sagging
position...*

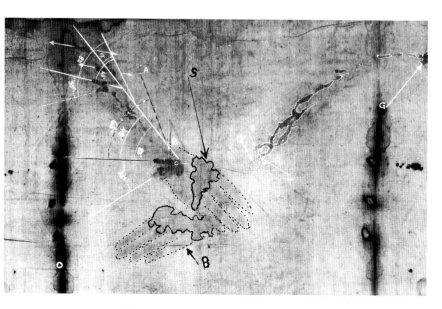

The rotary movement of the forearms around the nails caused these large bruises in the metacarpal crown or upper part of the hands (S) to the left and (B) to the right.

Bearing these facts in mind, it is clear how the back of the hands, which came into contact with the rough surface of the cross-piece during the rotary movement, received contusions (and maybe lacerations). This also explains the slight difference in the position of the two contusions, that on the left hand being found mainly in the area of the index and middle fingers, and that on the right being spread over most of the back of the hand, but in particular in the area around the little and ring fingers. The forward movement of the body had different effects on the two hands because of the different angles caused by the shifting of the body to the right.

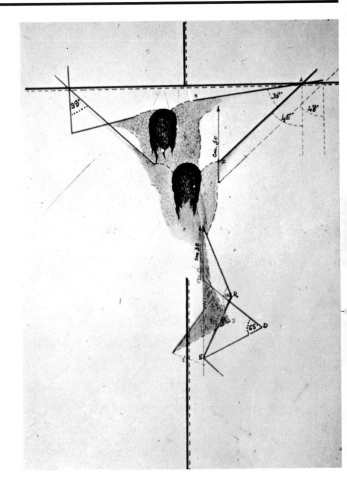

Axonometry of the two main movements of sagging downwards and raising up in the case of this crucifixion

St. John, who was present at the death of Christ, gives us a valuable piece of information when he says that Jesus in that supreme moment "bowed his head and gave up his spirit" (Jn 19:30). It would have been physically impossible for a man hanging *mainly* from his arms (the sagging downwards position) to move his head noticeably forward, since it would have been immobilized by the flexed cleidomastoid muscles. Thus the Gospel gives us an indirect supporting piece of evidence on the raised up position of our Lord in that final moment. This also explains how at the moment of death Jesus could cry out with a loud voice, something quite impossible for a person dying through asphyxiation. The evidence of the Holy Shroud is most helpful here: the fact that the Man of the Shroud is shown fixed in the final raised up position is in full accord with the medical details given by St. John and the Synoptics about the *"bowed head"* and the *"loud voice."*

Blood and saliva coming from the right side of the mouth

However, before this "loud voice" the Gospel gives us other words spoken by the Lord.

A careful examination of the Shroud reveals another interesting detail connected with this raised up position: *the shifting* of the whole body, naturally including the head, *to the right.* Clear proof of this is given by the blood which flows down the length of the right forearm (which was thus almost vertically bent), gathering at the elbow and by the three open wounds from the thorns on the forehead; there is also the trickle of blood from the *right* side of the mouth, which is of particular interest to us because of the fact that the mouth had opened to speak, with the moving result we now see.

Let us for a moment picture the "open, bleeding mouth," as described by St. Bridget *(Rev.* VII, 15), closing our eyes and concentrating on this detail: when we open them and look at the Shroud we will see that the mouth has now been respectfully closed, after the head was bowed forward onto the chest; it is no longer open to speak words of eternal life; but how many things are said by that blood and saliva which flowed sideways from the mouth and with their gentle flow accompany the last divine words of the testament of Jesus:

"Father, forgive them"…. *"I am thirsty!"* (Jn 19:28)

"Woman, behold, your son!... Behold, your Mother!" (Jn 19:26-27)

"My God, my God, why hast thou forsaken me?" (Mt 27:46; Mk 15:34)

"Today you will be with me in Paradise!" (Lk 23:43)

"It is finished!" "Into thy hands I commit my spirit!" (Jn 19:30; Lk 23:46)

The fact that the head was bent can be demonstrated simply by measuring the linear distance from the line of the mouth to a line across the body at the sub-mammary region on the frontal imprint on the Shroud. If we subtract from this the 18 cm. (7 inches) of the chest, we arrive at the sternoclavicular joint. This leaves us barely 9 cm. (3½ inches) in a linear measurement, or 7 cm. (2¾ inches) as a direct distance between there and the mouth…. This distance would be the measurement of that piece of cloth brought up against the chin as far as the edge of the mouth, and explains the touching detail of the head bent even in the tomb. The normal linear measurement from the mouth to the sternoclavicular joint, with the head upright, is between 17 and 19 cm. (6¾ and 7½ inches), and this measurement would be lengthened in the imprint by about 12 cm. (4¾ inches) as the sheet was brought up against the neck.

The imprint on the Shroud shows us a head with no neck, exactly like the *mandilia* of the seventh to eleventh centuries,[1] whose inspiration for the portrayal of the face of Christ was drawn from the Holy Shroud.

This all agrees fully with, and confirms, a detail recounted by the Evangelist, who speaks of Jesus dying after bowing his head (Jn 19:30). *Rigor mortis,* which would have set in immediately after death, would have prevented the disciples and holy women from forcing the head into an erect position on the ledge in the tomb.

1. Cf. M. Green, O.S.B., *"Enshrouded in Silence,"* Ampleforth Journal, LXXIV (1969), pp. 319-345.

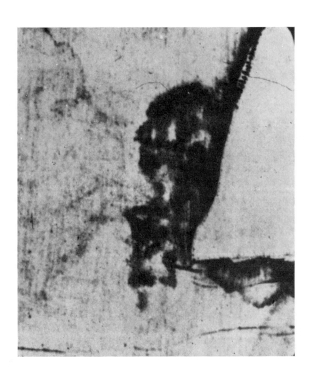

The wound in the side: at the top is the spear wound (4 cm. or 1½ inches) from which there flowed out blood and water; on the Shroud we see the blood which clotted on contact with the air, surrounded by the serous fluid.

Jesus Dies on the Cross

Execution by crucifixion, as reconstructed by a close study of the Shroud, has revealed not only a static reality (a wrapped corpse) but also the remarkable dynamics of the movements which the Man of the Shroud had to undergo in the course of his agony in order to avoid asphyxiation. It shows us the movements of sagging downwards and raising up, and opens a new field for medical investigation on the cause of the death of

By subtracting 18 cm. (7 inches) for the chest, we are left with 9 cm. (3½ inches) from the mouth to the sternoclavicular joint; the way in which the Shroud was wrapped over the chin reduces the linear distance to 7 cm. (2¾ inches) which is correct for a head bowed on the chest.

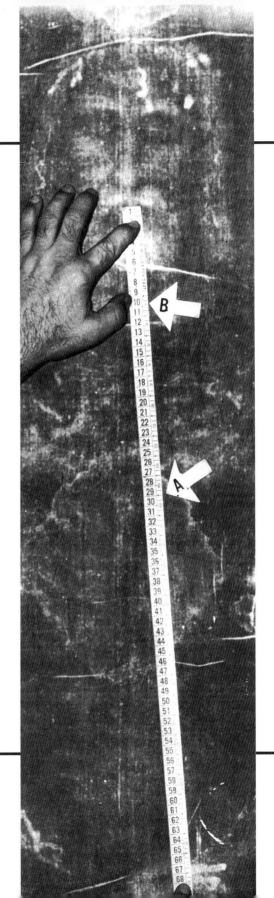

the Man of the Shroud, who is clearly identified with Jesus, the Man-God, who suffered under Pontius Pilate. The Man of the Shroud did not simply hang from his hands, but, pressing on the nail in his feet, he was able to lift himself up; his feet were nailed when his legs were in a bent position, so that he could push his body upwards in order to avoid asphyxia, which would otherwise have taken place after about ten minutes, as noted by Dr. Hyneck in descriptions of Austrian and German prisoners punished by being suspended by the hands from a bar.

But there is still more: St. John, who was present at the execution on Calvary, has given us what amounts to a real medical report when he says that "one of the soldiers pierced his side with a spear, and at once there came out blood and water" (Jn 19:34). It should be borne in mind that Jesus was fully conscious until the last moment, and that his death was a sacrificial death constituting the expiatory type of sacrifice which in the biblical conception took place through the shedding of the blood of the victim.

Not all the immediate causes of death suggested are in accord with the evidence given in Holy Scripture. This is the judgment we must pass on the diagnoses of asphyxia and traumatic shock, which always produce loss of consciousness and an irreversible state of coma in those dying from such causes.

This must be completely excluded in the case of Christ who in that last moment of life—the most precious for all humanity—offered himself up to the Father, crying out this offering and accepting death in full, free and loving conformity with the will of the Father. Other solutions, such as traumatic serous pericarditis or other serous disorders, do not seem to agree with the detail of the "blood and water" which flowed from the side of Christ *immediately* and *separately*.

Experiments carried out in Seville[2] show that if, two hours after death, a knife is violently thrust (as was the soldier's spear) into the undamaged heart of a corpse, there is never a clearly distinguishable outflow of blood and water. All this justifies further research into the physical cause of the death of Christ.

---

2. Dr. José Riquelme Salar, *Examen medico de la vida y Passion de Jesucristo*, Madrid, 1953.

Did Death Occur Through Hemopericardium?

A famous nineteenth-century Scottish doctor[3] can be credited with having carried out the most interesting research on well-documented cases of people who died through hemopericardium (or heart rupture). This could offer an adequate explanation, in terms of medical science, of the passage in St. John which states "and at once there came out blood and water," and thus reveal the cause of our Lord's death, which had taken place about two hours earlier.

Stroud's research, even though it was carried out in an era in which the medical nature of coronaries was not known, is valid nonetheless, since his observations were made only a few hours after death.

In these cases blood swelled the pericardiac sac in such a way as to eliminate the pleural cavity, and when the pericardium was opened with a scalpel the blood, even after only an hour, appeared already clearly divided into two elements: the plasma, because of its lighter specific weight, was at the top; and below was the corpuscular sediment. Thus Stroud posits the hypothesis that Jesus died through heart rupture. Medically speaking, this hypothesis is in agreement with the *immediate* and *distinct* outflow of blood and water as described by St. John.[4] Also, in certain well-documented cases, those dying through heart rupture gave a loud cry and died one or two minutes later.

In the case of Jesus, death was preceded by a loud cry, and then, bowing his head, he gave up his spirit. The loud cry, which cannot be reconciled with a theory of death by asphyxiation, fits a diagnosis of heart rupture, while the fact that he bowed his head suggests a raised up position of the whole body—and this is confirmed by a geometrical study of the Shroud. The soldier's spear thrust thus revealed a remarkable state of affairs when it occasioned the separate outflow of blood and water. If the heart had been undamaged before being struck by the spear, the blood would have mixed with the "water" in the pericardium, flowed into the pleural cavity, and then (and not immediately, as stated by St. John) have flowed out of the wound in the side.

3. William Stroud, *A Treatise on the Physical Cause of the Death of Jesus Christ*, London, 1847.
4. Professor U. Wedemissow, *Ipotesi sulla causa fisica della morte di Cristo*, Atti del II Congresso Internazionale di Sindonologia, Turin, October 7-8, 1978.

On the Holy Shroud the outflow of blood and water from the side, and the fact that the head was bent, are clearly shown.[5] The outflow from the side appears as a group of dark colored bloodstains, around which appear halo-like areas caused by serous fluid: this corresponds perfectly with the "blood and water" of St. John.

Today there are several competent doctors who maintain that acute ischemia of the heart can be the primary cause of rupture. The agony of Gethsemane could have been the stress factor which initiated myocardiac infarction, leading eventually to definitive rupture, which occurred along with the fissuring of the wall of the heart affected by necrosis.

5. See previous note. The priestly calendar found in Qumran would allow the necessary time span.

G. Ricci: "Crucifixion"; sculpture in wood according to research carried out on the Holy Shroud (Assisi, Pius XI Pontifical Regional Seminary)

"**I**t was the day of Preparation and the sabbath was beginning.... Now a man named Joseph...of Arimathea...a member of the council, a good and righteous man...went to Pilate and asked for the body of Jesus. Then he took it down" (Lk 23:50-53).

Thus it was already sunset when Joseph went to ask for the body of Jesus. Under Roman law, the family and friends of an executed man were permitted to give the body an honorable burial. Having assured himself, through the centurion, that Jesus was dead, Pilate granted Joseph the body for burial.

They must have removed the nail from the feet, lifted the crossbeam down with Jesus still attached to it, taken the nails out of the hands, and then carried the holy body to the nearby tomb which Joseph of Arimathea had made available for Jesus.

The Holy Shroud, with its own language of blood, reveals two details which allow us to make an accurate reconstruction of this sorrowful journey to the tomb.

The first piece of evidence concerns the area of the kidneys, where the body of the Man of the Shroud is marked with blood trickles running in a crosswise direction. These lead one to think of an outflow of blood caused by

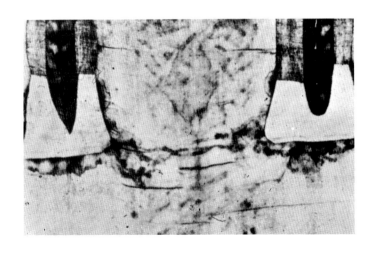

Outflow of post-mortal blood in the kidney region, caused by the horizontal position of the body after the descent from the cross

the horizontal position of the holy body on the journey from Calvary to the tomb.

The coloring of this blood, rich in *plasma*, is such that it can be analyzed as the "effect of the post-mortal sedimentation of the red blood corpuscles in the cardiac cavity, pierced by the spear" (Dr. Giordano). It is natural that, with the body in a supine position, blood from the lower part of the body would flow out of the wound in the side. This blood, which would still have been in the blood vessels after the wound in the side (while the blood in the upper part of the body poured out immediately following the opening made by the spear), poured out freely and left the characteristic marks which can be seen in the kidney region.

A second, even more moving piece of evidence can be found on the feet, particularly the left heel: fingerprints from one of the fortunate bearers of the body of the Lord. These prints were caused by the blood that would have flowed out of the hole in the feet, which had just been freed from the nails, due to the oedema occurring either before death through circulatory insufficiency or after death through hypostasis (Dr. Giordano). The blood ran down and concentrated in the area of the heels, where it left some unusual marks which allow perfect reconstruction of the hands to be made, with the fingers bent and tensed, showing the effort needed to carry the weight. The little finger, and the ring and middle fingers of the left hand, in contact with the heel, were surrounded by the blood running down from the hole in the left foot. The same thing happened with the right hand on the right heel, though the imprint is less clear.

Thus, it is clear from the Holy Shroud that the bearers of the body carried it to the tomb feet first.

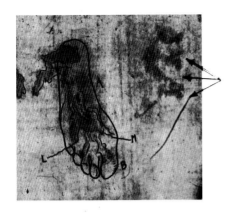

Left heel of the Man of the Shroud with the imprint of three fingers.

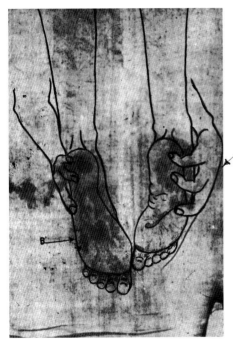

By carefully following the edges of the imprint, this picture can be reconstructed. It shows the little finger and the ring and middle fingers of a left hand, in a tensed position, typical of someone supporting a weight. In order to strengthen the grip, the thumb and index finger are naturally placed on the top of the foot.

"**N**ow *in the place where he was crucified there was a garden, and in the garden a new tomb where no one had ever been laid. So, because of the Jewish day of Preparation, as the tomb was close at hand, they laid Jesus there"* (Jn 19:41-42).

"And [Joseph] rolled a great stone against the door of the tomb, and departed" (Mt 27:60).

"It was the day of Preparation, and the sabbath was beginning" (Lk 23:54).

The disciples had only one hour in which to carry out the burial of Jesus— from sunset to the appearance of the three stars.[1] At least half an hour must have passed between the granting of Joseph's request to Pilate and the return to Calvary, having bought a shroud in a shop in Jerusalem. In the remaining half hour everything had to be completed: the nail had to be removed from the feet, the crosspiece lifted down, the holy body lowered, the two nails in the hands removed, the body taken to the nearby tomb.[2] There it was quickly arranged and laid on the ledge where the shroud had already been placed lengthwise. It would have been hurriedly bound and sprinkled with spices (following Jewish custom), and then the large stone was rolled into place in front of the entrance.

At this point, according to the testimony of St. Luke, the three stars were already shining in the sky (like the lamps in the windows of the houses of Jerusalem). It would have been necessary to hurry home, since the final

1. At Jerusalem on 14th Nisan of that year (785 of Rome), the sun set at 18:08 hours, while the last of the three stars, which indicated the beginning of the Sabbath rest, appeared at about 19:08 hours.
2. In Jerusalem, there were cemeteries for the bodies of executed men when they were not requested by relatives. If the family did request the body, both Roman and Jewish law granted this request, although according to Jewish law the body had to be buried in a tomb where no one else had been buried—as was the case with Jesus (Lk 23:53)—so as not to contaminate the bodies of the just. Only after the flesh had been reduced to dust could the condemned man be considered "purified," and the remains exhumed and buried in a common tomb. This is what happened to John of Ezechiel, whose remains have clearly been exhumed and buried in the little cemetery at Giv'at ha – Mivtar. In fact, according to Professor Nicu Haas himself, anatomical and anthropological research confirm that the bones were arranged in some kind of fixed order, a type of regrouping in general use at re-burials. The normal usage was to put the corpse in the coffin, and later collect together the bones for re-burial in an ossuary after the decomposition of the flesh (p. 38). It is also interesting that in some cases the longer bones were found on top in the ossuaries, still tied together with the intertwined stalks of plants, or with withered bunches of flowers or intertwined ears of corn (p. 38).

trumpet blasts from the Sabbath Porch of the Temple announced the beginning of the Sabbath rest.

Thus, there was no time for a complete burial. However, when death took place on Friday evening, the law allowed the ceremonies to be postponed until after the feast.[3] This is why, at the end of the Sabbath, the women bought spices to anoint the holy body. They would first have washed it seven times, then the hair and beard would have been cut. After this they would have anointed it and wrapped it in the Shroud, having first dressed it again.

The condition of the Man of the Shroud, unwashed, naked, with his well-combed hair and his beard, is not in disaccord with Jewish custom. It is merely that this custom was not completely carried out because of lack of time, for Jesus rose again before the burial could be completed.

Intentional Arrangement of the Shroud— His Mother Tends Him for the Last Time

The portion of the Holy Shroud which was to receive the back of the body of the Lord was laid on the ledge in the tomb, and the other half was folded down over the whole of the front of the body from the head to the tips of the toes. It was then hurriedly arranged around the various parts of the body and temporarily tied, awaiting the final burial which, in fact, never took place.

The most significant points of this intentional arrangement, which has left clear signs on the imprint, are the following:

The amazing imprint of the wound in the side, between the fifth and sixth ribs, shows the entire extent of the outpouring of the "blood and water." We would not have had this imprint if the Shroud had simply been *laid on* the body of the Man of the Shroud: to prove this, one has only to think of the position of the arm, folded over the mesogastrium, and hence close to the wound, as well as the natural curve of the hemithorax, to come to the conclusion that only an *intentional* arrangement of the sheet could have caused the formation of this marvelous imprint, somehow allowing us a clear vision of the fifth wound of the Savior.

Further proof of this arranging of the Shroud is found in the abnormal

---

3. Cf. *The Universal Jewish Encyclopedia,* "Burial," p. 496.

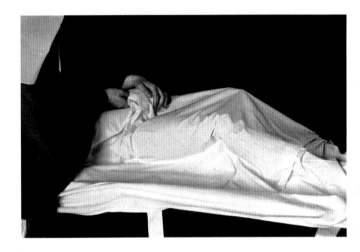

*The sheet is arranged around
the left hand, which lies
on top of the other*

shape of the *lower outer* part of the *right* forearm, as well as a lengthening of this forearm by about 20 cm. (nearly 8 inches) due to the folds in the Shroud produced when it was tucked over the left hand lying on top. There is consequently a break in the path of the blood on the right forearm as it flows from the wrist down to the elbow. This break alone has added about 7 cm. (2¾ inches) to the imprint of the forearm.

As well as this arranging of the Shroud in the region of the heart, there is evidence of two more: (1) one is the fold made on the inner side (mesogastrium) and outer side (pubes) of the hands, which were laid one on top of the other; (2) the other is the arranging around the left hand, which was on top, and this had the effect of considerably lengthening the imprint of the right hand lying below.

(1) In order to show just how much the sheet was arranged around the overlapping hands, we can point to the indisputable fact of the excessive distance on the imprint between the mouth and the wound on the left wrist.

In the light of what has been said (p. 57) concerning the head being bent forward on the chest and the position of the hands laid one over the other, it is

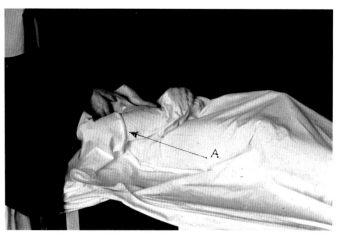

Tucking the sheet inside the forearms produced a fold in the material (A) and consequently...

...a break (A) in the path of the blood down the right forearm

a simple thing to check experimentally the distance in a straight line between the line of the mouth and the left wrist: the measurement on the Shroud (about 68 cm. or 26¾ inches) far exceeds any normal measurement, being about 20 cm. (nearly 8 inches) more than the average measurement taken from individuals between 1.62 and 1.83 meters (5 feet, 4 inches and 6 feet) in height. The vertical extension of the imprint caused by this arranging of the Shroud is between 16 and 20 cm. (6¼ and 8 inches).

(2) But a closer examination of the imprint of the right hand can show us a further example of his Mother's careful attention, which resulted in a lengthening of the imprint of this hand. If one thinks of the overlying left hand with its thumb drawn over into

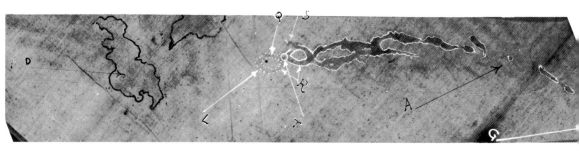

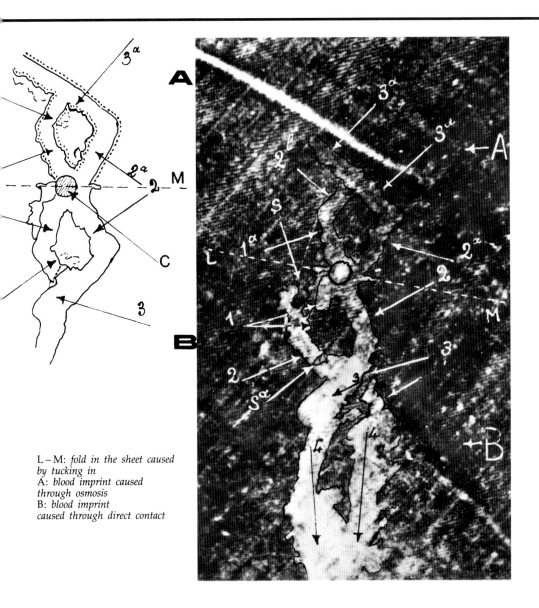

L–M: *fold in the sheet caused by tucking in*
A: *blood imprint caused through osmosis*
B: *blood imprint caused through direct contact*

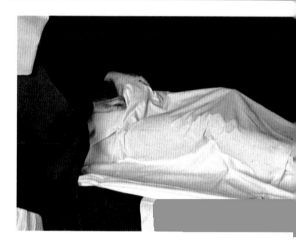

*With the left hand lifted up,
the sheet was tucked in as far
as the nail hole in the hand lying below.*

the metacarpal region, the thumb would be resting on the wound in the right wrist below. The Shroud was brought up to this wound by lifting the overlying left hand slightly, thus producing a fold in the cloth (L-M). This is shown by the duplication of the diamond-shaped patch of blood with rounded corners; the nail wound is clearly visible at the point where they touch (R).

The morphology of these two diamond-shaped patches shows direct contact in the one which goes from the nail wound toward the forearm (nn. 1, 2, 3), while a paler, but perfectly identical imprint was produced (through osmosis) in the case of the other one (nn. 1a, 2a, 3a). Measurements also indicate arrangement and folding of the Shroud at this point. Together, the two "diamonds" are about 5 cm. (2 inches) in length, which, added to the 4 cm. (1½ inches) of the slope of the left hand with the thumb moved over, and to the 2 cm. (¾ inch) of the curve of this same hand on the little finger side, give us about an 11 cm. (4¼ inches) extension in the imprint of the right hand. These 11 cm. (4¼ inches) added to the 6 or 7 cm. (2½ inches) of the fold in the Shroud around the area of the heart, and to a 3 cm. (1¼ inches) extension to the fingertips (due to the folding of the sheet under the fingertips so that the balls of the fingers appear as extensions when the sheet is stretched out flat) clearly show the excessive length of the imprint of the right forearm, which is shown as 62 cm. (24½ inches) on the Shroud. 62 cm. − 20 = 42 − 17.5 (the length of the hand) = 24.5 cm. (the ulna); or 24½ inches − 8 = 16½ − 7 (the length of the hand) = 9½ inches (the ulna).

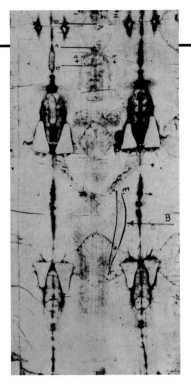

Effect of the arranging of the upper side of the sheet and the tucking up of the lower part: the imprints, indicated by the two curves, match each other

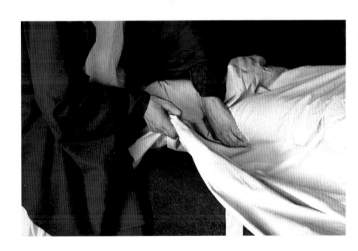

Tucking the sheet around the right femur

Tucking in around the right femur: this action (illustrated on the right) may well throw light on one of the details that can be seen on the photographs of the front and back of the body imprinted on the Shroud, in the area of the right femur. (Note that the right side of the body was the side more easily subject to his Mother's tending, since it would have been on the outer side of the ledge in the tomb.)

In these photographs the two imprints in this area are shown to match, leading one to think that the top side of the sheet was tucked in and then covered by turning up the lower side: now that the Shroud is laid flat, it would appear that the front side of the femur extends outwards—there would have been a larger area of contact here, owing to the tucking in, and the back imprint of the femur has a blank.

This is an action that mothers perform when swaddling their babies—how many times must the Virgin Mother have done it joyfully to the infant Jesus! Now she repeated the action, in sorrow, on those limbs marked by the whips and fixed in death.

A further sign of this intentional arranging of the Shroud is provided by several blood marks clearly visible in the area of the feet and situated beyond their anatomical position, on the outside of the right and left heels. The sides

The sheet was tucked in under the sole of the foot from the outside and around the outer side of the heel

of the feet were covered in blood which had flowed from the hole from which the nail had been removed. During the final moments of the burial, the sheet was clearly tucked in and folded back on itself, given the surplus length of the cloth at this point. Thus the blood mark extending from the right foot can easily be explained, as also the fingerprints on the left foot, which are mainly to be found on the outer side of the foot.

A further point should be mentioned: the tucking of the sheet around the body, which finds striking proof when the tibial area is measured. These measurements from the frontal imprint alone would appear to indicate that the Shroud was arranged on the lower part of the tibias. This arrangement must have consisted of the folding of the material across its width several times, owing to the surplus length of cloth at this point. It produced an apparent abnormal elongation (about 14.5 cm. or 6 inches) of the imprint of the tibias. In fact, the *dorsal* imprint of these same tibias (an imprint which is *unbroken*) gives a measurement of 36.4 cm. (14¼ inches), while the front imprint is about 51 cm. (20¼ inches)—which would be anatomically pos-

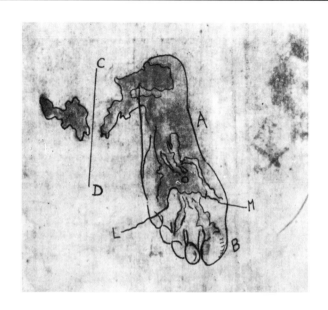

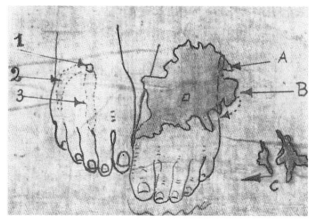

The effect of this arranging of the sheet can be seen in the imprints of blood beyond the feet: C – D and C.

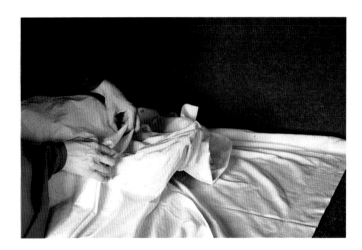

The sheet must have been folded laterally in the lower third of the tibias...

...causing an apparent elongation of the tibias: A – B C – D (AB larger than C

sible only for a modern giant. However, the front imprint is broken in the lower area, and there are traces at the sides which would appear to be the remains of powdered substances deposited in a liquid solution in the folds of the cloth as it was being folded; the solution, having dried, now appears as shaded patches to the naked eye.

That this may well have been the case is suggested by the fact that, during the fire at Chambéry in 1532, when the Holy Shroud was folded in the silver casket, the heat from the fire produced, apart from the well-known burn marks, those small dark patches, exactly level with the lower third of the tibias and coinciding with the two lateral folds already mentioned. In a laboratory examination, these might well show the presence of relatively large quantities of aloes and myrrh, substances which are known to be sensitive to heat.

Practically the whole of the imprint on the Shroud shows the care taken in arranging the sheet over all parts of the body—not over the whole *surface*, of course—particularly where there were wounds, swellings, and blood marks.

Given that the Mother of Jesus was present in the tomb, who else could be responsible for this intentional arranging? And without this motherly attention we would not have had an imprint so eloquent in its details.

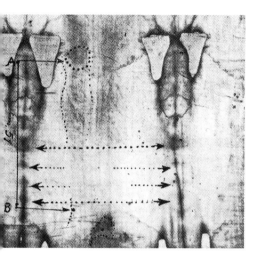 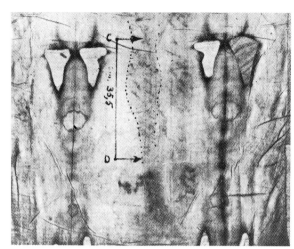

"The Sudarium Which Was on His Head" (Jn 20:2)

Is it possible from the Shroud to reconstruct the actual position of the abdomen of the Man of the Shroud as he lay on the ledge in the tomb?

Contrary to what is generally thought, the abdomen was not stretched out, almost parallel to the table, but was curved forward.

The anatomical proof of this can be found in the position of the hands of the Man of the Shroud, which lie over the pubes; at the same time, the left shoulder, which is higher than the right, shows the final raised up position of the body on the cross, as well as the crucified Man's movement to the right.

Rigor mortis fixed this unusual position, as can be seen from the dorsal imprint.

With a corpse in this curved position, it was natural not to place the sudarium on the face, but to put it on *(epì)* the head *(tès kephalès)* from where it would fall over the face. With the theory that the head of the Man of the Shroud was in an upright position and was thus lying flat on the ledge in the tomb, it would not be explained why St. John did not use *ópsis* (face) instead of

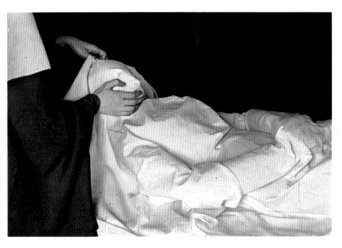

Covering the face with the Shroud; the fold at the top corresponds to the epicranium gap as shown on the Shroud.

They wrapped him with spices in linen cloths....

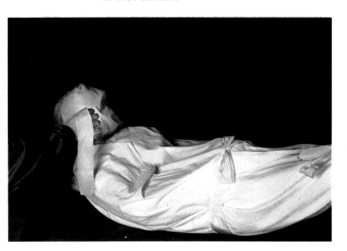

kephalès (head), since in this hypothetical position, the face would offer itself for covering by the sudarium.

In normal cases, after the seven ritual washings and the dressing of the corpse in its own clothes, the sudarium was either put *around* the uncovered face (as was the case with Lazarus) or *over* it. Here, however, the face was already covered by the Shroud, which served as an unusual garment for this naked corpse (the soldiers on Calvary had taken his clothes for themselves, drawing lots for the robe).

The Shroud, already placed under the body of Jesus, must have been unfolded from behind the neck onto the top of the head, then over the face, before being slowly drawn down as far as the ends of the feet: at this point Jesus' friends stopped pulling out the Shroud. However, owing to the length of the cloth, a certain amount (about 13 cm. or 5 inches) was left at the top of the head (the so-called epicranium gap); this piece, the ends of which coincide with the front parietal suture, was thus left without any imprint. This fact may lead one to think that it was an intentional act, designed to allow a further gesture— one as solemn as a holy rite—i.e., the last kiss on the face of the corpse. One could simply have lifted the Shroud at this point and then replaced it, as we would have done ourselves. Thus, it was enough to take up the extra part of the cloth over the head, bring it over the cranium arch, from the occiput to the front parietal suture, letting the small excess folded part fall back.

The imprint on the Shroud agrees with this reconstruction; if the surplus cloth had not been arranged in this way, we would have had an immediate duplication of the imprint of the head in reverse, in the sense that from the forehead to the sinciput and beyond there would have been a continuous frontal imprint on the Shroud, extending from the imprint of the face.

At this point, all that remained was to cover the head with the sudarium and draw it in at the neck with the bandages. This would have helped in the formation of the complementary front and back imprints of the head, matching each other, as we have seen.

Besides this, a close look at the photographic reproduction shows, immediately above the forehead (Z), a blood mark (a blow? a thorn

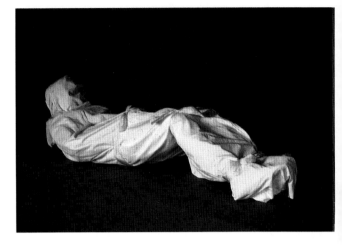

Thus wrapped, he lay for 36 hours in the sealed tomb.

Between the front and back imprints of the head there is an area (Z–Z¹) with no imprint—the epicranium gap.

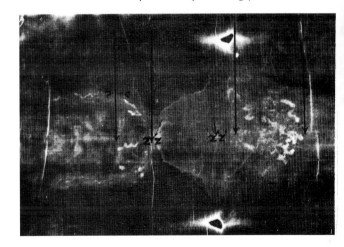

81

from the crown?), which in the present reconstruction would be repeated at the point Z^1 which, when the Shroud was folded back, would have been directly above the blood mark.

A pillow? At this point we should ask ourselves whether the head of the Man of the Shroud lay directly on the ledge in the tomb or not. The Shroud can provide us with information on this unusual item of research: (1) the curved abdomen and the bowed head, and (2) the marvelous imprint of the occiput, with the eight wounds and the resultant trickles of blood. At first sight, these two features are mutually exclusive: the occiput of a bowed head, with the abdomen slightly curved, and fixed in *rigor mortis,* will never touch a flat table, unless the table is considerably raised at this point, or unless a cushion or something similar is used which would allow the sheet to adhere perfectly around the convex shape of the occiput; note that there are twelve trails of blood around the occiput, over an area of about 13 cm. (5 inches), which have transferred perfectly, the transfer of clotted blood is not possible without prolonged physical contact.

Archeology can justify the theory of a raised piece of stone at the end of the ledge where the head lay. The other possibility—the pillow—is suggested by general compassion, and it may have been part of the funerary linen bought by Joseph of Arimathea and Nicodemus. (The sudarium was also found in the tomb after the resurrection, but it is not expressly said that it was bought, since it was only an accessory; the shroud and the spices—the principal elements—were the important things.)

Thus, without deviating from Jewish usage, but rather taking it into account without any preconceptions, and situating it in the exceptional circumstances, the Shroud of Turin, in its various facets, accords marvelously with these customs and undoubtedly bears eloquent witness to them.

Pictorial reproduction of the
face on the Shroud

RICCI G.
29.-VI.-1968 Koó A.

"**M**en of Israel, hear these words: Jesus of Nazareth...you crucified and killed by the hands of lawless men. But God raised him up... because it was not possible for him to be held by death. For David says concerning him, '...Thou wilt not...let Thy Holy One see corruption....'

"Brethren, I may say to you confidently of the patriarch David that he both died and was buried, and his tomb is with us to this day. Being therefore a prophet, and knowing that God had sworn with an oath to him that he would see one of his descendants upon his throne, he foresaw and spoke of the resurrection of Christ, that he was not abandoned to Hades, nor did his flesh see corruption. This Jesus God raised up, and of that we all are witnesses" (St. Peter in Acts 2:22-25, 27, 29-32).

The large round stone is still sealed at the entrance to the tomb, while the soldiers are on guard outside.

Jesus, having taken up his life again and being free of the laws of space, passes invisibly through the red rock streaked with white—the most glorious tomb in history.

When the dazzling angel of the resurrection rolls back the stone at dawn, to the amazement and terror of the guards, the linen cloths and the sudarium folded separately and lying on the ledge in the tomb are, with the simplicity of the works of God, the first eloquent witness that the glorious body was delivered from the sepulcher by divine power and not by thieves.

This is how the linen cloths appeared in the tomb of Joseph of Arimathea to the first official witnesses of the resurrection of Christ—Peter, the visible head of the Church, and John, the favorite disciple—when they first looked into the tomb at dawn on that Sunday; and it was St. John himself, an eyewitness, who handed down the memory of it in his Gospel.

There is, though, another witness that can be examined concerning this miraculous event: *the Holy Shroud*, that wrapped the holy body, covered in pre- and post-mortal blood (the former already clotted, and the latter partly dried).

Because of the biochemical laws governing the coagulation of blood and the phenomenon of fibrinolysis, we are able today to ask whether the morphology of this blood, clearly visible on the Shroud, conforms with the known laws of coagulation, and whether the 36-hour period of contact between Shroud and body was sufficient in that atmosphere to admit of the phenomenon of fibrinolysis as it appears on the Shroud.

We are dealing here with evidence which could not have been thought up by a hypothetical forger, since the phenomenon of clotting and the subsequent transfer onto cloth cannot be imitated by the artist's brush, which cannot reproduce the morphology of clotted or set blood.

In the authentic photographs, the imprints of the pre-mortal blood, which has transferred on the Shroud, appear thus: on the borders of the blood mark the fibrin has formed a thicker line, while inside the mark the plasma appears more faded, according to its natural color.[1]

With the post-mortal blood, which is especially evident on the Shroud at the wound in the side and in the blood which flowed from this wound down to the kidney region, and to some extent in the blood on the soles of the feet, we find dried blood corresponding in its morphology to blood which has not clotted previously and which, unlike clotted pre-mortal blood, shows grumes surrounded by serous fluid.

Trickles of coagulated blood
on the left wrist

At this point the Holy Shroud can be called upon as a witness to the phenomenon of hemolysis and fibrinolysis. When this occurs, it follows precise laws related to the time of contact. Thus, if a certain number of hours have not passed, the transfer onto the cloth does not take place, or does so only very roughly. However, if the period exceeds this number of hours, the transferred blood swamps the cloth through exces-

---

1. Cf. the wounds on the cranium, which are an example of this morphology (p. 11 above).

sive softening of the fibrin. This process has been demonstrated.[2] Furthermore, aloes and myrrh are hemolytic.

Now it must be said that the Shroud, which was in contact with the naked, wounded body of the Man of the Shroud, shows signs that the process of fibrinolysis was interrupted if, in the view of experts, the imprints are typical of coagulated pre-mortal blood and dried post-mortal blood, perfectly transferred and clear in their respective morphologies.

If this process did not continue to the end, there must be a plausible reason. There are two possibilities:

1. That the body was stolen after being once more stripped naked;

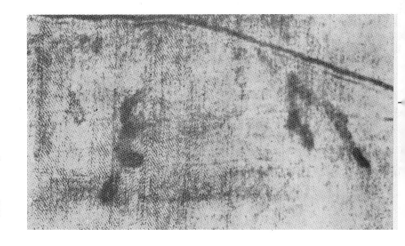

Trickles of blood in the center-right area of the forehead. In this photograph the blood, in the opinion of doctors, shows clear characteristics of clotted blood transferred through fibrinolysis.

2. The first experiments were made by Vignon. Recent discoveries concerning the liquefaction of blood clots under certain conditions may throw light on this problem. Dr. Black writes: "The phenomenon of fibrinolysis in subjects who have undergone extreme stress is now well documented. Clots formed on the skin before death can easily undergo fibrinolysis after death, either due to the action of tissue fibrinolysins or bacterial action. Clots that have been softened by fibrinolysis may be absorbed by linen, and experiments can be carried out to determine their morphology." Found in: Dr. D. Willis, "Did He Die on the Cross?" *Ampleforth Journal*, LXXIV (1969), pp. 27-39, p. 29, note 31.

2. That after a certain number of hours the body removed itself of its own volition, leaving to biological science of the twentieth century the privilege of revealing the secret which seems to be hidden in this holy sheet, a secret which may be intimately linked with the greatest mystery of human history—the resurrection of Christ.

The first theory, that of theft, was sketched out by the Sanhedrin, to the jingle of coins, and found no following among the first authentic witnesses of the risen Christ, nor in the early apostolic and post-apostolic tradition. Also, the linen cloths, found well folded and separate by the first official inspectors, Peter and John, at dawn on Sunday, would point to the theft of the body stripped naked once more—an inconceivable thing to the Jewish mentality of that time, according to which anyone in possession of, or merely touching, the winding sheet of a corpse was "legally impure."[3] It would also be against Roman law, under which violation of a tomb was punishable by death.[4]

In this hypothetical case, biochemical examination of the phenomenon of fibrinolysis would have to confirm that the robbers had removed the Holy Shroud from the body after a certain number of hours. On the other hand, the Gospels state that the soldiers were at the tomb from Saturday evening until Sunday morning; thus, if theft did occur, it would have to have been *before* the

---

3. *"Qui tetigerit immundum super mortuo, immundus usque ad vesperum"* (Lev 22:4-6).

4. In this case, the robbers, according to the Sanhedrin, were the "friends of Jesus" who wanted to prove that he had risen.

   However, it tends to be forgotten that Jesus' friends, at the time these events were taking place, had not the slightest idea of the resurrection. It was only after the numerous appearances of Jesus (two in the Last-Supper room behind locked doors, at the lake, etc.) that their faith was strengthened and they were able to make of this historical fact, which they themselves had witnessed, the central feature of the preaching of the Church. From these appearances behind locked doors they were able in some way to understand the very nature of the glorified body.

   Thus the theft of the body would have been a dangerous action out of all proportion to the purpose—that of trying to prove a resurrection in which they themselves did not believe.

   None of the disciples of Christ was charged officially with being the "desecrator"of that tomb, which was closely watched by temple guards who would not have hesitated to capture the "courageous" (!) desecrators and hand them over to the Sanhedrin if they had tried to remove the heavy stone, which was blocked by iron bars which, in their turn, had been sealed to that same rock out of which the cave had been hollowed.

   The disciples showed what their "courage" amounted to both before and after the passion of the Master, as we can see clearly in the Gospel (Jn 20:19; Mt 26:57; Mk 14:50).

tomb was sealed on Saturday at sunset. However, this could not be so, since the presence of the body would have been checked before the sealing took place. Moreover, the short time between the sealing (Saturday night) and the resurrection (dawn on Sunday) would exclude any possibility of negligence on the part of the soldiers in guarding the tomb, and thus any possibility of theft. This story of theft was invented by the Sanhedrin after the flight of the soldiers, who were frightened by what had happened. Still less can we believe the only other possibility that the theft would have taken place *inside* the sealed tomb and under the eyes of the temple guards!

If we wish to put forward the theory of serious negligence on the part of the Sanhedrin (which is also most unlikely) in not having checked the presence of the body of Jesus at the time they sealed the stone that Joseph of Arimathea, the owner of the tomb, had rolled over the entrance on Friday evening, we must conclude that the theft took place (if it took place at all!) during the Sabbath rest (!) or, at the latest, at sunset on Saturday, i.e., when, at the end of the Sabbath rest, the Sanhedrin hurriedly gathered to discuss with Pilate the question of posting guards at the tomb.

In this case the period the Holy Shroud was in contact with the body would be reduced by many hours if the theft took place on Saturday, or by at least eight or nine hours if it took place immediately at the end of the Sabbath rest (always supposing that the robbers wasted precious time in stripping the body and carefully folding the linen cloths, when at any moment they could have been discovered and severely punished, as Eusebius and the early Fathers of the Church observe). If this is what happened, examination of the fibrinolysis process would demonstrate a reduction in the precious hours of contact with the Shroud.

There is yet another possibility—that of the body being stolen while still wrapped in the Shroud. In this case, either the areas of the Shroud in contact with the wounds would have been shifted and the fibrinolysis process interrupted (as in the preceding hypothesis), or else, if the cloth did remain in contact with the blood, the number of hours of contact would be considerably increased and the morphology of the imprints would inevitably have suffered the consequences of excessible softening and spreading of the blood in contact with the cloth. This did not occur in the case of the Shroud of Turin.

It is no good, either, to cite Jewish theology, as has been done recently, on the occasion of the discovery of the remains of John of Ezechiel, and say that Jesus, like Moses, would have been buried in a hidden place, unknown to

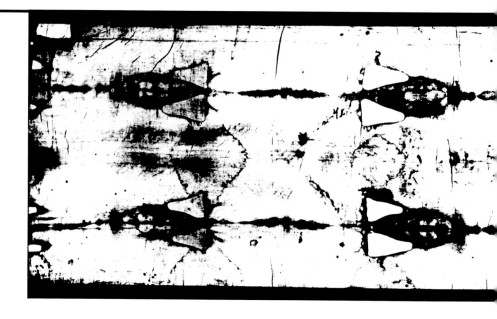

This linen funeral sheet (4.36 × 1.10 meters, or 14 feet, 3³/₄ inches × 3 feet, 7¹/₂ inches), with herringbone weave, is the most eloquent "corpus delicti" available to scholars in their reconstruction of the criminal action it contains: death on the cross. It is that of a man who before being condemned to death was subjected to a particular kind of scourging, and to a curious crowning with thorns (never recorded by historians in the case of other crucified men). His right hemithorax is marked by a spear wound, and he was wrapped naked in the Shroud without being washed and anointed with resinous oils. The faint imprint would suggest that this body did not undergo decomposi-

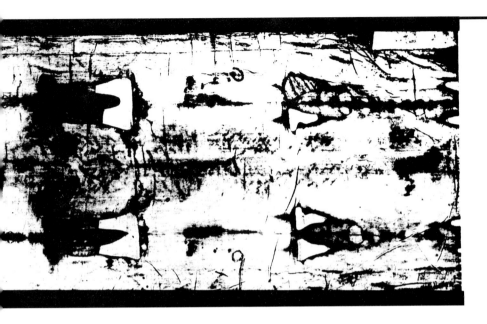

tion, which would have inevitably affected the condition of the Shroud. As arguments against the proposition that the body of the Lord was removed by the disciples, we have, besides the testimony of the evangelists, the examination of the nature of the blood imprints which, as the Shroud shows, comprise blood from both before and after death, the former having clotted and the latter having set. Both types of blood have been transferred exactly according to the process of fibrinolysis, and within a fixed period of time: about thirty-six hours' contact—the number of hours which, according to the Catholic faith, Christ was in the sepulcher before the resurrection.

anyone, and that his body could never have been found. This is simply a rather indelicate way of perpetuating the hypothesis that the body of Jesus was carried off by the disciples (and therefore buried by them in a hidden place); in this case the Shroud of Turin could not possibly be authentic, since it would have undergone the same fate as the body.

However, in refutation of this theory, we have the testimony of St. John, who says that the burial clothes were found carefully folded separately from the sudarium (which was also carefully folded) on the ledge in the tomb at dawn on the Sunday of the resurrection. This testimony would exclude the authenticity of any other shroud, connected with other contradictory and absurd theories, which are discredited by the evangelists and patristic tradition.

This then is the Holy Shroud, with its unmistakable imprint like that of a photographic negative, with the morphological characteristics of blood imprints that only modern biochemistry has discovered—characteristics that cannot be imitated with a brush, even by the cleverest medical men today. These imprints have a carmine-mauve coloration which recent experiments have shown to be possible because of the presence of aloes and myrrh in the cloth, since usually blood absorbed by cloth in time completely loses its characteristic coloring and fades to a light sepia color. This then is the Shroud, the imprints of which were perfected by various chemical reactions, such as that of the aloin, all of which contributed to producing in this funereal sheet the moving image of a man condemned to death on the cross, the sentence carried out with nails and preceded by a characteristic scourging and by a very exceptional crowning with thorns, and then, in order to make certain of death, struck with a spear through the right side of the thorax (instead of the customary breaking of the legs). The image is of a Man whose head remained bowed even in the tomb. These details correspond only with Jesus of the Gospels.

We then come to the imprint of the face, which is truly remarkable: its renaissance beauty, revealed for the first time by the photographic plate in 1898, could not possibly have been thought up and painted in negative by the brush of some painter in an age preceding the discovery of photography.

All of this has the value of testimony, written in letters of blood on that sheet which wrapped the body of the Man of the Shroud for about thirty-six hours—testimony which is linked indirectly, but genuinely, to the only miracle, yet the most tremendous of all, worked by Jesus for his own sake, in fulfillment of his solemn affirmation: *"For this reason the Father loves me, because I lay down my life, that I may take it again. No one takes it from me, but I lay it down of my own accord. I have power to lay it down, and I have power to take it again; this charge I have received from my Father''* (Jn 10:17-19).

His resurrection was thus the crowning glory of his mission on earth and a prelude to his glorification in heaven—that of the head and the members. St. Paul was to proclaim this solemnly for all people: *"If Christ has not been raised, your faith is futile.... But in fact Christ has been raised from the dead, the first fruits of those who have fallen asleep. For as in Adam all die, so also in Christ shall all be made alive. But each in his own order: Christ the first fruits, then at his coming those who belong to Christ''* (1 Cor 15:17, 20-23).

This final meeting of the resurrected Christ with "those who belong to Christ" completes the mystery of universal salvation, as he brings us to the Father and the Spirit, like a most precious trophy torn from the hands of Satan.

The souls of the just of the Old Testament, who waited for him, have already received his liberating presence, as has "the little flock" of the New and everlasting Testament who, during the forty days of the founding of the Church—his reign of love—experienced his radiant visits: the first of all to meet him was Mary of Nazareth, his Mother, then Mary Magdalene, the holy women, Peter, the apostles, and the disciples.

Since his ascension into heaven in the flesh, Christ has encountered every generation of the faithful, and will continue to do so until the final resurrection of the chosen when, by divine grace, even our bodies will be glorified in his likeness.

Thus, from this inviolate tomb sprang the means of universal glory; we have received a pledge of this in the grace of faith that comes from Baptism and from the sacraments of his Church, as a precious seed that Christ will take back for himself on the day of our meeting with him, if the seed has borne the fruit of good works worthy of the Father. "Then every man will receive his commendation from God" (1 Cor 4:5). "And so we shall always be with the Lord" (1 Thess 4:17).

"We adore thee, O Christ, and we bless thee, because by thy holy cross thou hast redeemed the world.''

I. Prior to the Scientific Tests of 1978

Between the first phase of the burial, hurried and incomplete, of a bloodstained body which there was no time to wash and oil, and which remained unclothed, and the second phase of the burial which should have taken place, but in fact never did, there occurred the phenomenon of the fixing of the imprint on the Shroud.

The Shroud imprint, frontal and dorsal, face and body, is to be attributed to the blood (both pre- and post-mortal), aloes and myrrh, humidity, and to the contact of the sheet soaked in these latter substances with the bloodstained body.

This contact took place because of intentional, loving arranging of the sheet around the face and body, covered with diverse foreign substances—blood, sweat, dust, spittle on the face, etc.—capable of influencing the imprint on the sheet. In this connection the recent experiments of Rodante and Baima Bollone are most interesting. They correct—experimentally—Paul Vignon's famous theory. Vignon considered that the imprint on the linen was essentially due to ammoniac vapors given off by the corpse through the slow, continuous evaporation of the remains of febrile sweat, rich in urea, which was deposited on the surface of the skin, and of water vapor due to the natural loss of humidity from the body of deceased persons; according to his theory, the aloes and myrrh on the funerary sheet reacted with these substances, producing ammonium carbonate. The vapor from this substance, in the humid atmosphere (humidity given off by the corpse) created in the space between the body and the sheet, stained the sheet in direct proportion to the contact with the wrapped-up body. Where there was less contact, the imprint is fainter. This theory is known as the vaporigraphical hypothesis.[1] The weak point in Vignon's theory—at once noted by Dezani in 1933[2]—rests in the considerable quantity of urea required to

1. Paul Vignon, *Le Saint Suaire de Turin*, Masson Ed., Paris, 1938, pp. 5-7, 22-37.
2. Dezani, "La Genesi della Sindone di Torino," *Gazzetta Sanitaria*, 1933, p. 124.

Face of Christ. Oil painting by an anonymous artist of Urbino react in such a way as to imprint so extensive a surface as that of a shroud; further, one must point out the unjustified presupposition of the uniformity of the presence of this substance over the whole of the body. What is more, as Professor Baima Bollone[3] so rightly observes: "Evaporation—from a corpse—is a phenomenon of a so-called negative-consecutive nature, closely connected to the phenomenon of hypostasis, such that one would be obliged, if accepting Vignon's theory, to presume a differential emanation from the various (epistatic and hypostatic) parts of the corpse, producing imprints of varied aspect and intensity. Basically, the over-rapid acidification of the cutaneous and subcutaneous tissue of the corpse, along with the differential evaporation in the various anatomical regions of the corpse, do not permit us to accept as a matter of course Vignon's hypothesis, at least that part of it which postulates the formation of an ammoniac from the urea and the subsequent action of this latter and the modification of color resultant from the aloes."

The tests and experiments conducted by Baima Bollone (cf. *art. cit.*) have now made it possible for us to draw some reliable conclusions concerning the aloetic imprints of the anatomical parts, either from the physical features or from trickles of blood and clots present on the epidermis of corpses.

It has been confirmed that it is entirely possible for a simple mixture of aloes and myrrh in a humid atmosphere to leave indelible imprints of a corpse on cloth. These imprints change in character with the passage of time; the contrasts are accentuated, and this is especially evident on the photographic negative of these imprints. "Even the briefest of exposures (45 sec.) of material soaked in the aloetic mixture to the face of a corpse with traces of dried blood produces an imprint which, although hardly visible to the naked eye, is clear on the photographic negative and also when it is observed with light behind it. In these conditions the viewer is struck by the presence, with clear contrasts, of hematic traces."[4]

Professor Rodante also reached similar conclusions. He obtained imprints very similar in their nature to those on the Shroud, noting, however, that they were more perfect—that is to say, corresponded better to the model of the Shroud—if a damp sheet was used.

The origin of the imprint is the focal point of discussion. To solve the

3. Baima Bollone, "Rilievi e considerazioni medico-legali sulla genesi delle impronte sulla Sindone," *Sindon*, XIX, n. 25, pp. 10-16.
4. Cf. Baima Bollone, *art. cit.*, p. 15.

problem it is certain that spectral and microanalytic examinations employing an electronic scanning microscope and a mass spectrometer would be most useful,[5] as would be some specific examinations to verify the presence of blood, etc.[5] Indeed it seems to us that the origin of the imprint is to be considered entirely within the realm of normality, and that it is not correct to hypothesize, as do some,[6] a certain "incandescence" produced at the moment of the resurrection.

As has been recognized by all major students of the document in this century, the entire imprint of the Man of the Shroud **is characteristic of a deceased person,** who is moreover in a marked state of *rigor mortis.* Thus the Shroud is a document of the passion which leaves us on the threshold of the resurrection.

Nor is it any longer possible to affirm what Carreño quotes from Professor Judica Cordiglia (cf. below), that "one is forced to affirm the impossibility of reproducing imprints by any means whatsoever." Actually, as we have seen above, **the contrary is true.**

The morphology of the blood on the holy Shroud evidences two types of blood: pre-mortal blood, shed *intra vitam,* characterized by the fibrin halo around the edges and by the light plasma in the center; and post-mortal blood, shed *post mortem* (e.g., that from the wound in the side), characterized by the opposite effect—a halo of plasma on the outside, and fibrin in the center.

These two morphological characteristics of the blood reveal that the imprints on the Shroud are not the work of a forger, who could not have known, all those centuries ago, this data concerning the process of clotting, nor the fibrinolytic process which made it possible for hematic substances to be transferred onto the cloth in a period of approximately 36 hours of contact with the body, thanks to the hemolytic action of the aloes and myrrh.

Scientific research can be applied to the Shroud in many different ways, and this is precisely because science today has many resources, ranging from ultramicroanalysis of a fragment of linen thread to the electronic elaboration of pictures first translated into a code; pollen, spores and minerals can reveal with certitude the place in which the object in question originated or was at one

5. The usefulness of these tests were stressed by Msgr. G. Ricci and Dr. E. Patrizi, of The Roman Center for the Study of the Holy Shroud, at the 1st Holy Shroud Conference in Albuquerque (USA), in March 1977, in complete agreement with the American Scientists. An official request was jointly presented to the Turin authorities on September 19, 1977.
6. E.g., Carreño Exteandia, *La Sindone ultimo reporter,* Ed. Paoline, Alba, 1977, pp. 15 and 135-137.

time found; the "enhanced photographs"—that is to say proportionally intensified pictures—give us a glimpse of invisible or almost invisible details, now perceptible to the naked eye; carbon-14 dating will soon make it possible to date even minute portions, etc.

Thus, many tests could yet be made on the Shroud; and we hope that they are carried out, for they will enrich our studies for many years. For example, if the examination of an area of the imprint as small as even the end of a hair can be carried on with an ion-microprobe (a microprobe using an ion current) we will be able to obtain analytical chemical confirmation of the theory we are about to propound.

In the meantime it is well to bear in mind various facts: the hypothesis of, and thus the search for, red globules as such is absurd a priori, since the components of blood are very prone to hemolysis, and then the hemoglobin which was previously contained within them becomes diffused in the surrounding area and the structure (*stroma*) which contained it is left like an empty shadow. Thus the question put to the scientific members of the 1969 commission for the study of the Holy Shroud of Turin was *per se* inadmissible, since it is well known—as a member of the commission, Professor Zina, said—that "morphological investigations—I mean those concerned with research on corpuscular elements of the blood and in particular the erythrocytes or red globules—carried out on hematic traces rarely have positive results after a relatively short space of time."[7] The reason for this is found in the fact that **"even a negative result does not permit us to deny the presence of blood in the material under examination,** since various factors can influence the state of conservation of the constituent elements, altering their morphology and color and thus preventing their precise presence from being confirmed."[8]

Hemolysis can easily take place even with a small degree of heat, and can be induced, for example, with saponine, liver salts, or simply a solution of sodium chloride—45% to start the process, reducing to 33% or 30%. (And undoubtedly the whole surface of the skin of the Man of the Shroud must have

7. A. Zina, "La Sindone: Ricerche e studi della Commissione di Esperti nominata dall'Arcivescovo di Torino, Cardinal Michele Pellegrino, nel 1969," in *Suppl. Rivista Diocesana Torinese*, January 1976, p. 57.
8. C. Gerin, *Medicina Legale e delle Assicurazioni*, II, p. 415.

been covered with saline crystals caused by abundant perspiration.[9]) But of more immediate interest to us is this: it now seems that, contrary to what was once believed, hemolysis is not due to simple chemical factors, but to external causes, such as the difference in osmotic pressure within the red globules and in the plasma. In fact, unequal distribution of ions can cause the red globules to swell, even causing them to burst or hemolyze. Now myrrh, for example, being a resin, favors this exchange of ions (both the positive cations and the negative anions); thus calcium ions may be replaced by sodium ions. To summarize: for a variety of reasons, not all of which are yet known to us (partly because, even though the kinetics of hemolysis have been studied since 1897, our knowledge of this phenomenon is still incomplete), we can assume that **on the Shroud it will be possible to distinguish only the simplest trace elements which were once contained in the red globules and the plasma**— e.g., iron, sodium, potassium, copper, etc.

For this reason—and bearing in mind the various historical vicissitudes undergone by the Holy Shroud—it is essential to remember the words of some other members of the 1969 commission of experts. Professors Frache, Rizzati and Mari stated: "The negative result of the investigations carried out does *not* permit an absolute judgment denying the hematic character of the matter under examination."[10]

With the information and knowledge now at our disposition, we consider highly improbable—to say the least—the theory of light or heat radiation caused by the resurrection (a theory held by Carreño, Wilson and other writers) for two reasons:

(1) It is clear and can be demonstrated photographically and electronically that **there are different densities** on the different parts of the imprint;

(2) It is known and has been proven by various persons that the imprints on the Holy Shroud darken under particular circumstances of light and heat, which would indicate—while we await the necessary confirmation of chemical analyses—the possible presence of aloes, which is extremely light-sensitive and of hemato-porphyrins.

Furthermore, it can be shown that contact played a vital role in the origin of the imprint from the fact that those parts of the sheet which were not in

---

9. Perspiration can vary between 0 and 200 grams per hour, and contains 99% water and salt.
10. *Op. cit.*, p. 54.

contact, or were only in very light contact, either have no imprint or have such a faint one that it fades to zero.[11]

This can be seen, for example, on the face in the areas of the eye sockets, the sides of the nose, the sloping part of the left cheek and also on the right cheek where, owing to the swelling level with the side of the nose, there seems to have been no contact either between the right cheekbone and the swelling, or between the swelling and the right side of the mustache. Again, there appears to be no imprint, and thus to have been no immediate contact with the sheet, between the mustache and the chin, i.e., to the sides of the lower lip; the same absence is attested around the swelling in the center of the forehead.

Therefore the imprint is not a *miracle*, but rather the result of a series of circumstances which caused various biochemical reactions. Of particular interest is the photo-sensitivity of aloin (a substance found in aloes in a proportion which varies between 5% and 25%, depending on the type of aloes). Bearing in mind that aloin becomes darker under the action of light and air, we may suppose that some light—a lamp inside the tomb—filtered through the mesh of herringbone cloth: we would then certainly have an imprint in which those parts of the body in higher relief—and thus most exposed to the light—would be darker and clearer while the parts in lower relief would receive less light and thus be less clearly defined. This hypothesis, which was put forward by the American Accetta,[12] would explain the "negative" nature of the background imprint, the way it fades to zero, and its three-dimensionality (i.e., the fact that information of a three-dimensional nature is included in it).

However, we still have to explain the "positive" transfer of the blood trickles onto the Shroud. In this opinion the most important point to be considered is fibrinolysis (resoftening of coagulated blood due to the fibrinolysis in the blood or to bacterial action), which is well documented and more noticeable in those subjects who died in conditions of violent stress. It was fibrinolysis which permitted the perfect transfer onto the cloth of the hematic substance which covered the whole body of the Man of the Shroud. This too is exceedingly complex and, like hemolysis, is helped externally by the aloes and myrrh, whereas, internally, fibrinolytic activity in the plasma is very high in a person who has multiple wounds and dies of infarction of the myocardium.

11. Contrary to what was said by the Jackson and Jumper in: "The Three Dimensional Image on Jesus' Burial Cloth," in United States Conference of Research on the Shroud of Turin, Albuquerque, 1977, Holy Shroud Guild, ed., 1977, pp. 74-94.
12. J. S. Accetta, *On the Image Formation Process of the Shroud of Turin*, priv. com., Dec. 1977.

Are we thus dealing with a combination of external and internal causes? This cannot be excluded.[13] What is certain is that the imprint on the Shroud could definitely not be the fruit of the mind of a hypothetical forger, and this for innumerable reasons: the phenomenon of the coagulation and subsequent transfer onto the fabric is in perfect accord with the morphology of blood which flowed *intra vitam* and which clotted (through a chemical process affecting the blood, whereby the fibrinogen forms a spongy web of fibrin which "darns" or blocks a wound, thus preventing further loss of red globules and gathering fresh ones together to form a scab) and blood which set or dried in the air, i.e., post-mortal blood.

We should remember that the imprints of living coagulated blood on the Shroud have the following appearance (which is made clear on the photographs taken in simple ultraviolet light and Wood-light and also from photographic transparencies): around the edges of the bloodstains the fibrin has formed a thicker halo, while in the center the plasma is lighter or faded. On the other hand, in the case of post-mortal blood (especially that from the wound in the side, and also in the region of the kidneys), we find dried blood, which has not the morphology of blood which had previously clotted but, unlike living coagulated blood, appears as clots of blood surrounded by halos of serous liquid.

This is the point on which the Holy Shroud can be called upon as evidence or indirect proof of the mysterious event that interrupted the fibrinolytic and hemolytic process at just the right moment to give us the wonderful imprint on the Shroud.

13. Cf. G. Ricci, "Risposta alla Prof.ssa Noemi Gabrielli," in *Osservazioni alle Perizie Ufficiali sulla Santa Sindone* 1969-1976, p. 72.

II. After the Scientific Tests (1978 – 1982)

In recent years (1969, 1978 and 1982) a new chapter has been added to Shroud studies due to the new, important, and, in my opinion, determining information brought to light by scientific research.

I shall provide a very brief summary of the conclusions of the principal researchers involved in the first Italian commission (1969) and the second American one (STURP—Shroud of Turin Research Project).

After the photographic studies of 1898 (S. Pia), of 1931 (G. Enrie) and of 1969 (G. B. Cordiglia), the first direct scientific examinations of the Shroud were those conducted autonomously in 1969-1973 by nine of the fourteen experts on the commission appointed by the Archbishop of Turin, Cardinal Pellegrino, guardian *pro tempore* of the Shroud, and by its actual owner, Prince Umberto of Savoy.

Their names and conclusions are as follows:[14]

1. Professor Cesare Codegone (Engineer), Director of the Institute for Applied Physics and Nuclear Installations of the Turin Polytechnic. With regard to the C-14 test for dating the cloth Professor Codegone concluded that given the present (1969) state of the art it would be wise to wait until the C-14 dating technique was perfected or replaced by a more trustworthy method.

2. Professor Enzo DiLorenzi, Head of the Radiology Department of the Mauriziano Hospital in Turin, concluded that radiologic examinations would not yield useful results; he believed that at best, since this type of examination would not alter the sample, it could prove useful if carried out directly on the Shroud if iron, chlorine and potassium were found in bloodstained samples of the cloth and if it were established by fluorescence spectroscopy that the amounts of those elements correlated with the composition of blood.

3. Professors Giorgio Frache, Professor of Forensic Medicine at Modena, and Eugenia Mari-Rizzati and Emilio Mari, also of Modena, carried out generic hematologic examinations limited to the ABO blood group system. The results were negative, although they did not rule out the hematic nature of the material under examination.

---

14. Cf. *Notes on the Official Expert Analyses of the Holy Shroud*, 1969-76, International Center of Shroud Studies, Via S. Domenico, 28, Turin.

4. Professors Guido Filogamo, Professor of Anatomy at Turin, and Alberto Zina, also of Turin, performed microscopic examinations and concluded that the light microscope examination did not reveal the presence of red blood cells, but that their formation could not be ruled out with certainty, although certain characteristics, such as dimensions and appearance of the granulations, led them to believe that it was unlikely. They concluded that more certain results might be obtained with the use of a scanning electron microscope directly on the fibers. Examination under conventional and electron microscopes established the absence of heterogeneous coloration or pigmentary material. They noted that the image (and the blood) had only penetrated the superficial fibrils. No comparative examination was performed to study the back of the Shroud.[15] High-power magnification showed that the image consisted of very fine yellowish-red granules forming part of the fibers themselves.

5. Professor Silvio Curto, head of Egyptology studies at Turin University, concluded after an initially negative examination that the cloth of the Shroud could date from the time of Christ, but that any more precise dating was not possible.

6. Professor Noemi Gabrielli maintained with regard to the origin of the imprint that it was an artifact produced by a printing technique and that it was the work of a great artist of the late fifteenth and early sixteenth centuries who used the shading technique of Leonardo.

The partial and uncertain conclusions of the members of the diocesan commission puzzled experts and elicited understandable reactions. In the meantime, while a team of American experts with sophisticated instruments was being assembled by the ingenious initiative of Fathers Adam Otterbein and Pietro Rinaldi, respectively President and Vice-president of the Holy Shroud Guild of America—a team that later would be given a mandate for an in-depth study—other valuable research was being carried out in palinology by the Swiss criminologist Dr. Max Frei, and in the field of manufacturing techniques by the Belgian Textile expert Professor G. Raes, Director of the Laboratory of Meulemester Voor Technologie Texstilstoffenrijks Universiteititgent.

7. Dr. Max Frei was given permission to apply sticky tape to the clear, non-image areas of the surface of the Shroud to remove samples of powder in November 1973, on the occasion of the first televised showing of the Shroud and during expert analysis of the official photographs that Dr. G. B. Judica

---

15. Only one edge was unsewn in order to photograph the weave of the cloth.

Cordiglia, Jr., had taken in 1969 (Dr. Frei was one of the experts, together with Dr. Spigo and Dr. A. Ghio). These samples led to the identification of the pollen of forty-nine species of plants from specific phytogeographical regions: sixteen species were found to be native to central and northern Europe; thirteen were from highly-saline halophytes very typical of or exclusive to the Negeb region or the Dead Sea; twenty were of other plants typical of the steppes of Anatolia, especially of the south-eastern region of Turkey, the north of Syria and the region about Constantinople—overall, three-quarters of the pollen originated in the Middle East, and one-quarter in Europe.

The Swiss expert's first conclusion was that the Shroud had been exposed in the regions of Palestine, then in Turkey and then in Europe.[16] Experiments proved that the pollen could not have been carried by the wind from Palestine to those regions, and certainly not to Europe. The pollen study did not support the hypothesis of J. Wilson that the Shroud had been in Cyprus, since M. Frei found no pollen indigenous to Cyprus, but only pollen from the Eastern Mediterranean which was common also to Palestine.

8. Professor Raes, 1976. A few square centimeters of cloth were cut from one edge of the Holy Shroud. This sample is described as a herringbone 3:1 twill weave which was particularly used for silk and linen, or highly-valued fabrics. The irregularity of the spinning and the weave itself suggest hand weaving. Thirty-meter rolls of linen produced on a vertical loom took two women a week's work.[17]

16. An interesting feature could be the discovery of traces of cotton fiber in the Shroud, which would indicate that it was woven on a loom also used to weave cotton. This could be in accordance with what was permitted by the ancient Jewish Code, if this was in force at the time of Christ, whereas there would have been difficulties in mixing wool (of animal origin) and linen (of vegetable origin), since such mixing of species was forbidden by the same Code. However, had the cloth been woven in the West, the presence of cotton threads (gossypium herbaceum), as some suggest, would date it prior to the fourteenth century (1352—Lirey), if cotton began to be woven in Europe only prior to the twelfth century in Holland, and from the eighth century onwards in Spain. This is always presuming that internal examinations (Carbon-14 or palinologic examinations, for example) were to prove such presumed Dutch (twelfth century) or Spanish (eighth century) origin. But we would then be faced with the question of how three-quarters of the pollen is indigenous to the Middle East. This is another point in favor of the theory of a Middle-Eastern origin of the Shroud.

17. Cf. Pietro Savio, *Ricerche sul tessuto della S. Sindone* (Grottaferrata: 1973).

STURP Studies—Shroud of Turin Research Project

It should be observed at the outset that the first examinations date from 1977 and that they were not carried out directly on the Shroud, but on the photographs taken by Enrie in 1931, and those taken with a Wood-UV light by G. B. Judica Cordiglia, Jr., in 1969. Dr. Lynn in Pasadena and the experts Jackson and Jumper in Colorado Springs were the first to use a computer to analyze the photographs of the Shroud. Having analyzed the image with a microdensitometer to establish variations in luminosity, or density levels, in the varying intensity of the images, Jackson was the first to find a probable correlation between the distance of the cloth and the body, assuming the Shroud was lightly draped over the corpse. Together with Jumper, he concluded that the Shroud image encodes three-dimensional information: this was shown with the use of the VP-8 image analyzer system, which verticalized the intensity of the shadows of the image. It also proved that the imprint of the Shroud image was not produced by painting, printing or mordants.[18]

Dr. Lynn also analyzed the photographs of the Shroud with a computer and thus contributed significantly to the "reading" of the Shroud imprint, helping in the identification of the Man of the Shroud,[19] although without bringing to light anything truly new.

18. Professor Tamburelli of Turin has perfected the type of research carried out by Lynn, Jackson and Jumper, and at the Second International Congress on Shroud Studies he confirmed the three-dimensional nature of the image, and revealed new traces of lesions that are invisible to the naked eye. Meanwhile, Professor Cacciani, of the Roman Center for Shroud Studies, and Lecturer in Physics at Rome University, has produced an electronically elaborated structure and shape of the trickles of blood and their innumerable residues that are invisible to the naked eye, and has come to the well-founded conclusion that the image of the face of the Man of the Shroud was formed by these.

19. When they were subjected to unidirectional derivation examination, Dr. Lynn's splendid photographs of the scourge marks on the back and front revealed the bifocal convergence of the scourge strokes, fully confirming our geometric examination. The photos also highlight a difference in the latitude of the two focal points, inasmuch as he points out a slight difference in height. This detail of a lower focal point (the right lower than the left) had suggested to some (to Barbet, for example) that one scourger was shorter than the other. I think that a more logical explanation lies in the different areas chosen by the two scourgers to strike. It can be seen that the right-hand scourger tended to concentrate more on the area from the buttocks to the legs, while the other struck the upper part of the trunk. The convergence point in each case was determined by the end of the forearm, which remained aimed towards the chosen area. However, this does not necessarily mean that the scourger in question was of a different height than the other.

Quantitative (Chemical and Physical) Study by STURP

The definitive results in the various fields of specialization were those of the quantitative studies carried out by American experts, who, unlike the Italian commission, had undertaken to issue unanimous official reports of the results only with the collegial approval of all the members of the STURP scientific team. The results were excellent on the whole, inasmuch as the direct examinations, which began on October 9, 1978, and were accompanied by microanalytical studies of specific areas of the photographic mapping of the Shroud, allowed for the convergence of various types of analyses (chemical, biochemical, spectroscopic, spectrophotometric, etc.) of the image, which will make it possible in the future to achieve a better understanding of the imprint on the Shroud and a more precise interpretation of the quantitative and qualitative correspondence of the various values of the elementary substances—quantity, density, distance and other variables that actually concurred in forming the imprint. This will thus make it possible to improve on the coordinates hypothesized by Jackson and Jumper, which are for the moment limited to intensity and presumed distance, and to obtain a still better three-dimensional image than that presented by the two experts at the Second International Congress of Shroud Studies on October 7, 1978.[20]

However, what we may consider to be a new and positive element is that three-dimensionality is a specific characteristic of the Shroud, as evidenced as well by the photographic negative of the Shroud imprint already familiar from previous photographs, which confirms the presence of an object with a volume under the sheet. This completely rules out the work of a painter, which would have produced a flat and distorted image, as was seen, for example, in the case of the beautiful pictorial reproduction of the Shroud by Reffo.

The following are brief summaries of the findings of the foremost experts of the STURP team:

1. 1978. Ray Rogers, of the Los Alamos Laboratory, a thermochemistry expert, was the first to use x-ray fluorescence to establish the presence of

---

20. Was the Shroud only draped lightly over the body? This was the hypothesis of Jackson and Jumper presented at the Albuquerque Congress in 1977. It was immediately challenged by the CRS because in the prior programming of the VP-8 no consideration had been given to the tucking in and folding that the cloth had been subject to at the final moment of burial. These tucks and folds are responsible for the fact that the imprints on the Shroud are not anatomically recognizable, and since these, in turn, were not programmed for the computer, the results are unacceptable even on an aesthetic plane.

pigmentation heavy metals. This is an absolutely critical test to prove whether the Shroud imprint is a counterfeit (painted) or not. The test would immediately have revealed the presence of pigments. The examination ruled this out definitively. Subsequent spectrographic and spectrophotometric examinations performed in selected areas gave quantitative proof of the presence of heavy atoms, localizing them on the "map" of the Shroud, and eliminating the possibility that they might be responsible for the image.

2. 1978. W. Miller, Professor of Scientific Photography and President of the Brooks Institute, was responsible for some splendid photographs. We would particularly note the visible transmission photograph which made it possible to discover and confirm certain data obtained from other microanalytic studies, such as the nature of the low density (7×100) of the Shroud image.

3. 1978. Professors J. Accetta and S. Baumgart of the U.S. Air Force Laboratory, Albuquerque. Infrared spectral reflectance test performed directly in Turin. Thermographic examination to discover any lack of homogeneity, or the accumulation of material on the image. Result: both examinations eliminated the possibility that the image contains non-homogeneous elements or visible artifices; in other words, the structure of the image as examined by spectroscopic reflectance and thermographic analysis does not present any mass or directional anomalies, as would have been the case if the image had been formed by a brush dipped in an artist's paint pigments. This confirmation is based on the difference in reflectance in the various points of the image, which vary between 3-4 mg to 8-14 mg per square centimeter. This is extremely small to hypothesize a painted image.

4. 1980. R. Morris, L. Shwalbe and J. London, experts in radiography, conducted x-ray fluorescence studies which revealed traces of calcium, iron and other elements typical of blood. Among the most interesting of the analyses carried out in 37 spectra, those on the bloodstained areas are particularly convincing, since they proved to be spectrographically similar to one another. This shows that they are not the result of paint spread on cloth but of a concentration of materials "absorbed" by the fabric.

5. 1980-1981. J. H. Heller and A. D. Adler's "chemical analyses" of materials removed from sticky tape samples lifted from specific areas of the Shroud were used to establish the presence of whole blood on the basis of the discovery of hemoglobin derivatives, bile pigments and protein. This was confirmed by a total of 12 tests.

One of the most interesting tests was the one employing proteases: a solution of enzymes used to dissolve proteins which leaves no residue. Red-coated fibrils from the Shroud, presumably due to blood and microscopic sherds from a "blood" stain were treated: the red coating disappeared, leaving white-colored fibrils, and the microscopic sherds of blood disappeared completely. Also very important was the protease test conducted on hematic substance taken from the scorched and burnt areas. In the first case they were of a brownish color, and in the second, black: the protease dissolved the proteins, leaving a residue of carbon, while the hematic substance of the scorched area dissolved, leaving a residue of coal, precisely because they were the residue of charred proteins.

After these experiments, anyone interested in the authenticity of the Shroud may be justified in wondering at the high level of ingenuity of an hypothetical forger[21] of the Shroud who, after the 1532 fire, would have had to apply intact blood with a brush only a few millimeters from charred and burnt blood residue.

Despite the fact that iron is found in various forms over the entire surface of the cloth, its presence can be explained in terms of natural processes and not as added pigment. There is no chemical evidence of the application of pigments, stains or dyes to the cloth in order to produce the image.

The chemical differences between the areas of the cloth with the image and those without indicate that the image was produced by some process that dehydrated the structure of the cellulose of the linen in order to produce a conjugated carbonyl group as a chromophore. However, an image-formation mechanism has not yet been identified which explains all the Shroud's properties.

The presence of three types of iron was confirmed: (a) a chelated form tied to cellulose; (b) forms tied to hemoglobin; and (c) ferric oxide (Fe_2O_3).

6. 1981. S. Pellicori and Mark Evans of the Santa Barbara Research Center, California. With a view to providing a spectral analysis of the imprint of the image of the body of the Man of the Shroud, filters were selected which would provide the best resolution of the highest contrast areas of the image.

21. When the Pope got word of the fire in 1532, rumor had it that the Shroud had been replaced by a skilled forger, since the original had been completely destroyed. Cardinal Gorrovedo was therefore appointed to ascertain the Shroud's genuineness, and although he did not have the scientific background of Heller and Adler, he limited himself to verifying what had happened and to an "optical" examination that was sufficient to guarantee the identity of the Shroud, as is stated in his official report (cf. *La Sindone Santa*, Doc. No. 11, p. 310).

Fluorescence, microphotographic and infrared tests have ruled out the hypothesis (McCrone) that the image was produced by paint pigments.

It has also been proved that blood is present in large quantities in the area of the chin and beard. The spectral examination has confirmed that the blood curve has a completely different trajectory than those of other stains: the characteristics of metallic porphyrin and of human blood protein in the image are proven by spectrographic analyses, which reveal denatured hemoglobin. The examination of the concentration of iron in the cloth is particularly conclusive and convincing: this element is distributed uniformly (3-4 mg/cm^2 over the whole cloth): iron absorbed by the linen flax in the bleaching stage; iron in the bloodstains (about 40 mg/cm^2 together with various elements typical of blood), and iron oxide that migrated after the 1532 fire and concentrated mainly through capillary action or osmosis near the edges of the water stains.

The microphotographic tests carried out by Pellicori on small blood incrustations revealed a color of recent, not old, blood which formed amorphous red-orange incrustations between the fibrils and in the fissures.[22]

Another detail that has come to light in the 500x microphotoscopy by Pellicori and Evans is the presence in the area of the left rotula and the tip of the nose of hematic substance with high-image density (which, however, did not go through to the other side of the cloth), mixed with a very fine powdery material in the fibrils which, due to its precise localization, leads to its interpretation as street dust mixed with blood from the relative lacerations and contusions suffered by the Man of the Shroud on the way of the cross.[23]

7. 1980. Roger Gilbert, Jr., and Marion M. Gilbert took UV fluorescence photographs which revealed a pale luminosity around the stains from the wrist

22. This fact caused interest and surprise. However, we should remember that the still relatively fresh hematic substance was "initially" in contact with a new sheet, one that had been recently bleached and was therefore rich in hemolytic substances such as saponin (Dinegar report). This substance would have had the capability of starting the hemolytic process, in turn blocking that of discoloration of the blood. In the 36 hours following burial, this process was followed by that of fibrinolysis, assisted by alkaline substances such as aloes and powdered myrrh, which accumulated other hematic substances on top of the hemolytic substance. We can understand how in the most intimate part of the two processes regarding this hemolysis the original orange-red coloration could be found. The amazement remains, but the explanation has been provided by organic chemistry and color microphotoscopy.

23. Cf. what was said concerning the binding of the arms to the crosspiece (p. 15), the tying of cord to the left ankle, the tying together of a number of condemned men, and the inevitable falls, and those impacts of the left knee and the face, particularly the nose.

joint,[24] the side and the feet, with a fluorescence similar to that of blood serum.

In order to discover "how" the imprint of the Shroud image was formed, an impressive array of optical and microscopic tests were conducted, including the majority of those summarized here, in order to examine blood components: infrared and radiographic thermography, Raman microanalysis, IMA (ion microprobe) examination, and scanning electron microscopy (Jumper, Mottern, *et al.*). There was general agreement as to the nature of the image as produced by dehydration and degradation of the cellulose of the surface fibers, producing a weak light reflection in the visible range (Pellicori, 1980). Only the most superficial fibrils of each thread in contact with the body are dehydrated, even in the darkest areas of the image, and no significant traces of pigments or inorganic chemical substances were found in the image, apart from certain isolated residues of colors (in two specific areas)—the work of artists who in the past had access to the Shroud for the traditional pictorial reproductions. It was concluded that the image was not painted (McCrone), printed or artificially superimposed on the cloth (Gabrielli). No definitive result was obtained which explained the image-formation mechanism of the imprint apart from the observation of the dehydration and degradation of the cellulose of the cloth as explained above.

8. The microanalyst Professor Giovanni Riggi of Numana, the only Italian scientist who was a member of the STURP team, made a perhaps determining contribution to the research by finding a substance chemically similar to natron in the vacuumed material aspired from the back of the Shroud—that is, from the external part of the sheet at the time of burial, and thus a substance that was mixed with the aloes and powdered myrrh that was generously sprinkled over the wrapped body, and, in my opinion, also on the funerary bench, under the Shroud and all around on the walls and on the ground.

The discovery of natron[25] (sodium carbonate) was important. Natron is a chemical compound which is common in nature and in normal use in the Middle East (among the Egyptians it was used to dehydrate corpses prior to embalming). It could have played a determining role in the dehydration of the

---

24. The first Wood-UV photographs taken by the official photographer G. B. Judica Cordiglia, Jr., in 1969 showed the same thing, although this phenomenon did not receive much attention and went unnoticed by many.

25. Together with that of the myrrh found by Professor Baima Bollone, and the traces of socotrin aloe observed by Fr. Frei.

linen fiber and formation of the Shroud image. It is the task of chemical research to hypothesize and carry out experiments to determine which substances—sweat, serum?—could have contributed to the reducing phenomenon that the experts unanimously agreed took place.

It may be relevant to recall a phenomenon now known for many years. It was noted by Barbet *(op. cit.,* p. 46), who is today hailed by scientists for his opinion that the origin of the Shroud body imprint was due to the reaction that as early as 1942 Volckringer had observed in the images of plants collected in old herbaria. After a relatively long period (at least thirty to forty years), the cellulose of the paper appears dehydrated, forming an image similar to a photographic negative. And, what may be even more interesting, electronic elaboration reveals a three-dimensional image.

All we have to do now is wait: perhaps this is the last stage in the fascinating journey of scientific research into the structural physical nature of the imprint on the Shroud.

It is by now accepted that the transfer of the hematic substance, whether coagulated or clotted, onto the Shroud can be explained through the presence of hemolytic and emollient substances on the cloth, such as saponin, aloes and myrrh. The presence of natron, which is revealed in high concentrations, completes the list of the substances that were certainly present at the time of that burial, and this points the way for research into the chemical reaction or chain of reactions that actually caused the imprint. At this point the only real mystery is no longer the actual imprint, which can be proved physically, but who was the person wrapped in the cloth. If it was not the Jesus of the Gospels, who else could it have been?

We would like to conclude this prospectus, which we have reduced to a minimum for obvious reasons, with the research of Professor Baima Bollone, President of the International Center for Shroud Studies in Turin.

This study is at the end of the list solely for chronological reasons, since the results of the precious research he carried out with his team were published almost contemporaneously with those of STURP. The following are two extracts from the press communique of Professor Baima Bollone, which summarize his important discoveries:

"Through the applications of the most sophisticated methods of forensic hematology, the use of a very modern microprobe-equipped scanning electron microscope revealed the presence of inorganic blood components in the same reciprocal percentage ratio as the bloodstains, and histochemical examinations revealed ferrous iron of biological origin. Proceeding by degrees, it was possible to identify hematoporphyrin traces which, together with iron, constitute the chromatic group of hemoglobin. Lastly, treating the material with acetic acid and sodium chloride, a characteristic crystalline precipitate was obtained made up of hemin (the well-known Teichmann's crystals), which forensic pathologists accept as certain evidence of the existence of blood in stains.... There was still the question of the biological species to which it belonged. Immunofluorescence studies were carried out in collaboration with Professor Anna Massaro and Dr. Mariolina Jorio of the AVIS of Turin. This research revealed that human globulins are still preserved in the stains on the Shroud, thus proving that the blood belonged to our species" (*Stampa Sera*, March 1, 1982).

"We continued our research with a view to learning more about the individual character of the human blood that had thus been identified.

"The problem of blood typing according to the ABO system was therefore considered. This system divides blood into four groups (A, B, AB, and O), which is distinguished in the first three cases by the presence of the relative erythrocyte antigen (or agglutinogens), and in the case of the O group by its absence. It should be noted that the blood serum of each of these groups contains the opposite natural antibody (or agglutinin), so that alfa agglutinin (or anti-A) is found in the serum of A blood, beta (or anti-B) in B blood, both alfa and beta are found in O blood, and there is no agglutinin at all in the AB group blood. The search for the anti-A and anti-B agglutinins yielded totally negative results, as would be the case for blood belonging to the AB group.... On the whole, the various examinations carried out lead us to the conclusion that the blood of the Man of the Shroud belongs to the AB group" (*L'Osservatore Romano*, January 12, 1983).

A Postscript to Scientific Research

Coins on the Eyes?

Even today in writings on the Shroud we still find references—and indeed with renewed insistence—to alleged evidence of coins on the eyes. It is claimed that such evidence has been shown by electronic elaboration of the imprint of the eyes of the Man of the Shroud. There are also claims that it was the resurrection that left the body imprint on the Shroud. These two opinions were never made official by STURP because not all its members accepted them.

The first theory gained notoriety in 1975, when the first VP-8 photographs by J. Jackson and Jumper were computer-processed and offered for the first time to the experts meeting at the Albuquerque Congress in 1977. It should be immediately noted that the image analysis was performed on the black-and-white photographs of 1931, in which, as we know, the contrast between density levels was already heightened, so that the VP-8 further enhanced it with the result in the figure below:

Any observer can see in the center of the eyes those circular, flat, raised surfaces, which appear to be two objects and which were thought to be the image left by two coins in relief. In a brief interval at the Congress, J. Jackson consulted the *Jewish Quarterly Review* of July, 1895, in which under the article "Beliefs, Rites and Funerary Customs," Part IV, by A. P. Bender, the custom of placing coins or pieces of pottery on the eyes is discussed; the article describes this as a custom among Jews in the Middle Ages, believed by ancient tradition to have been done in order to prevent the eyes of the dead person from opening before glimpsing the other world. After they had examined the computer-processed photographs, many of those attending the Congress felt it reasonable to conclude that this custom, which in the Middle Ages was taken to be an ancient tradition, had also been honored in the case of the Man of the Shroud.

Another reason adduced in favor of this theory was that if it was true that the custom of placing coins on the eyes of the dead dated from the first century and the Shroud bore very clear signs of such a custom, it followed that the Shroud itself must date from that period. This would be collateral archeological proof of dating which could render the use of the C-14 test unnecessary or at least not urgent—a test which until then had been called for by all parties but which had met with certain serious technical difficulties.

Barely two years later, in 1980, Father Filas, S.J., of Loyola University of Chicago, who had been present at the Albuquerque Congress and had read a paper on science and faith, thought that he could distinguish over the right eye of the Man of the Shroud a type of coin which he had found in a coin collection—the *lepton* of Pilate—and claimed to have discerned the traces of some letters of the words TIBHPIOU KAICAPOC from the exergue of the coin on the fibrils of the area of the eyes. The photograph offered to readers here is the original photograph of the electronic elaboration offered to me by Jackson himself, reduced by 6.15x from actual dimensions of the image of the face on the Shroud. If we take the circular imprints on the eyes as coins, it is not difficult to measure their diameter in order to obtain a precise measurement: all we have to do is find the relation to the real distance between the two folds of cloth framing the face, which in Enrie's original photograph is 23.4 cm. across. The small relief in the photograph of the presumed coin is 2.8 mm. in diameter, which, multiplied by 6.15, puts its diameter at 17 mm. As I have personally ascertained from the coin collection of the biblicist Monsignor S. Garofalo, Pilate's coin has a diameter of barely 14 mm., so that it would appear to be smaller than that imaged on the Shroud in the VP-8 elaboration.

We should also note the universal custom, Jewish as well, of closing the eyes of the dead, which was performed then as now with a simple gesture over the eyelids and was the first of a series of ritual gestures carried out in the course of a normal burial. Furthermore, the reason assigned for placing coins on the eyes is strange and should not be attributed to Jewish sensitivity and intelligence: once the eyes of the body were closed they would not open again, and if they in fact did reopen (in the case, say, of apparent death) a 14-mm.-diameter coin would certainly not prevent them from seeing the world again.

In the case of the Man of the Shroud, the orbits of the eyes, which were already closed, provide two small spherical surfaces on the Shroud that was placed over them, which have marked the cloth at the points of contact. At these points it is possible to see, under visible light, a very light, indeed almost invisible, darkening due to the (chemical) reaction of the organic substances present on the skin of the dead man (sweat, etc.), which, having been subjected to a first, and perhaps repeated, photographic study (Enrie, 1931), as noted, suffered a considerable increase in density. When this was then subjected to further electronic elaboration, the VP-8 verticalized the spherical edges of the small imprints, and with its orthogonal projection created the illusion of something solid in relief, like the traces of a small coin.

It should be considered that the placing of a Roman and decidedly pagan coin, considered "impure" by the Jews, on the eyes of Jesus,[26] would have been a matter involving religious principle for the Jews who performed the burial rite.

Moreover, from the morphological point of view, given the metallic nature of the coins, the least that would have happened to the Shroud imprint in this case would have been to prevent contact between the cloth and the skin, leaving two little areas of background color of the cloth without any impression, precisely because of the absence of any chemical reaction.

This elementary observation applies both to the hypothetical *lepton* of Pilate and to any coin of a larger diameter, even admitting that this theory—based solely on an opinion current in medieval Jewish circles—holds true for the first century as well, and in particular could be extended to the case of "Jesus of Nazareth."

Furthermore, even admitting that the minter mistakenly used a K in place of a C (two completely different letters) in the letters UCAI, which in fact formed the basis for the distinguishing of the Greek inscription of the exergue,

26. Especially when we know that this type of money was not allowed to be brought into the "treasury" of the Temple and that money changers were used in order to deal with this problem.

anybody can see that their circular disposition is out of round with the circumference of the alleged coin.

The "Flash" of the Resurrection?

It was precisely from the realm of physics that a clear indication was obtained, after the scientific fluorescence tests performed by R. A. Morris, L. A. Schwalbe and J. R. London directly on the Shroud imprint in Turin. The imprint was non-fluorescent. This meant ruling out any theory that entailed explosive radiant energy, thus of a thermal nature—even if limited to minute fractions of a second—as supporters of the radiant energy theory postulated regarding the energy released at the moment of Christ's resurrection.[27]

Had there been such a flash, this would have caused the Shroud imprint to fluoresce, since the radiance would have had a thermal nature. This can also be deduced from the claims of certain people with regard to the apparent "identical" color of the Shroud imprint and the light scorch marks seen on the edges of the burns from the 1532 fire. This apparent—or solely optical—similarity is unfortunate, as was confirmed in 1978 by the instrumental examinations, which clarified both the fluorescence of the scorched parts, which were found to be thermal in nature, and also the different density in coloration of the scorched parts and of the Shroud imprint, so that explanations of the origin of the imprint would have to be found elsewhere. Further proof was adduced by the transmission photograph produced by W. Miller, in which both the scorched parts and the blood are visible, whereas the imprint of the body—the intensity of which is a bare 7% when measured instrumentally—was not visible.

Regarding this theory, an explanation must still be given as to why the Shroud image—the imprint of which, according to this theory, would coincide with the instant of the return of the risen Christ to glorious life—should bear the very clear imprint of a face that may be serene and majestic in death, but undoubtedly has an ecchymotic appearance, with the head still bent onto the chest and eyes closed. The body is still marked by *rigor mortis*, completely bowed from the scourging,...and is not the body as it should have been at the moment of resuming the glorious life, with eyes open and face radiant—in other words, the body of the Living One.

27. ...Which would have blown away the heavy round stone at the entrance to the tomb, leaving the Shroud collapsed upon itself, intact...according to Ashe, Willis, Carreño, Fossati, and others.

BIBLIOGRAPHY

Eric Ponder, *Hemolysis and Related Phenomena*, Grune & Stratton, N.Y. & London, II ed. 1971, p. 398.

Giulio Ricci, *Questioni di Sindonologia: Risposta a Don Luigi Fossati*, Ed. Centro Romano di Sindonologia, Roma 1978, pp. 5-9.

VV.AA., "La Sindone: Ricerche e Studi della Commissione di Esperti Nominata dall'Arcivescovo di Torino, Card. Michele Pellegrino nel 1969," *Suppl. Rivista Diocesana Torinese,* Jan. 1976, pp. 55-57 and pp. 49-54.

VV.AA., *Osservazioni alle Perizie Ufficiali sulla Santa Sindone,* Ed. Centro Internazionale di Sindonologia, Torino, Jan. 1977, pp. 71-74.